SECRETS OF THE
GOLF WHISPERER

ON AND OFF THE COURSE

DAN DEMUTH

ISBN-10: 1497393671

ISBN-13: 9781497393677

Library of Congress Control Number: 2013908661
CreateSpace Independent Publishing Platform
North Charleston, South Carolina

Acknowledgments

Thank you to all the people who have supported me on the journey of writing this book.

To my wife and best friend, Andrea, for not only all her love and support, but for her analytical and creative mind providing me great feedback as she lives and believes in my work. She also has adapted the concepts in this book and applied them to her twenty-eight years in corporate America—not to mention her ability to play her own game on the course.

To Kathryn Harwig who spent many hours offering writing advice and assistance. If it wasn't for that playful round of golf and her ability to use her intuition, I may never have been able to finish this project.

To Jim Early my business coach, when I first started my business and throughout the years, his priceless coaching allowed me to learn who I am and believe in myself.

To the golf professionals that I worked with in my younger years who allowed me to see new possibilities through the experience: Craig Waryan, Fred Shoemaker, Tom Wilcox, Tom Shea, Michael Turnbull, Mark Neva, and John Schlaman.

To Jeff Ringhofer, for his countless hours of marketing support.

To Wes Hamilton, for his work with meditation, vision, and passion that helped me see new possibilities.

Certainly to all of my clients who have given me the opportunity to learn and grow along with them. It has not only been a great joy to observe their successes, but also to have gained up so many great friends along the way.

Dedication:

To my parents who gave me a great experience to live life with safety and challenge, and Heidi Kub (my niece) we lost you at such an early age.You certainly have taught many of us to live in the moment.

Contents

Introduction

The more I know the less I know.

What is it you really want out of life, work, or for that matter, your golf game, yoga, or other challenging activities etc…?

What drives your performance?

Do you feel that you are operating at peak capacity?

Have you had a preconceived notion of how to get better? Are you paying attention to what matters to you most? In business, personal goals, or golf/sports?

We can listen and not hear, touch and not feel, look and not see. We can struggle and work and strive but never reach our target. If you feel that way about your career, life, or sporting endeavors, you are not alone. Most people have never learned the art of optimal performance and reaching their target. Why? From the work that I have done over the years, there are probably as many reasons as there are human beings. But one of the biggest things that I have learned through golf is that we often try to fix what is going on only from what we see (grip, stance, and swing) before we know what we are thinking (do we have a target in our minds throughout the performance?). However, this strategy often doesn't work in helping people improve. We have a saying: "If there is no target, there is no coaching." The coach's job is to keep the individual, team, or group focused on a target. The golf swing or putting stroke often changes when a person is focused on the target throughout his or her performance. So, in other words, if the ball goes way off line and the swing looks terrible, be careful what you are trying to fix. I have realized that golf is a great medium for understanding vision and focus.

In recent years we have faced one of America's biggest recessions. Modern business leaders have become accustomed to making more out of less. Days are filled with meetings and appointments as the pace of business seems to get faster each day. Very few leaders think of spending more to engage their employees and customers in order to grow their businesses. They simply want to cut expenses wherever possible in order to survive. But, in reality, this is an important time to recognize the value of communicating within the organization to broaden the overall vision and clarify the intent.

I am very well aware that you may see this type of work as being nonsense, mystical, new age, or a bit too much fun when you have a big problem to be solved. **However, my experiences over the past quarter century have proven this type of learning works for CEOs, business leaders, executive teams, small businesses, and of course golfers.** I have seen companies triple their incomes within a two-year span. I have seen golfers lower their scores by thirty-five strokes in one year. Our mental abilities affect monetary performance in the office and affect our physical performance on the course.

Our perceptions of our lives have many forces that shape our experience, each having an impact on whether we feel good or bad. Most of these forces are out of our control, but the lessons of how you create your happiness and passion for yourself, your family, and your community can often be decided by how you choose to play the game.

Throughout my years as a golf professional, golf coach, business coach, and executive coach, I have come to realize that the core principles of golf are exactly the same as those needed for a successful business and a professional career. The reason most golfers are unhappy with their games is that, while they may have taken many lessons to learn "grip, stance, and swing," they have not been taught how to focus on a target.

In our business and personal lives, the same thing is true. This is why I began to explore the subject of creativity in a variety of corporate settings and small businesses as well as in my own continued personal work of being a creative golfer. In the course of this work, I began to discover that releasing individual and organizational creativity involved far more than just gaining new skills, discovering new ideas, and learning how to be a leader. I soon realized that the major portion of this work was about having my target/goals match my vision and how I could achieve my desired outcomes by playing them backward. I learned what my options are when something happens that is out of my control.

In grade school and high school, I was a top performer in golf. As I went on to college to learn more about the golf business and how to teach, my game became a mess. I do not blame the people who taught me, because "grip, stance, and swing" was all that the culture of golf knew to help someone improve at the time. In the 1980s and '90s, and in many cases to this day, the PGA workshops I attended were all about correcting what was wrong in a person's "grip, stance, and swing," rather than working on his or her thought process. As a result, I lost my own creative potential and got caught up in the "how to" rather than where I wanted to go. I now see this as a great opportunity to help others become aware of the possibilities in their games and businesses. The core principles of golf are exactly the same as those needed for a successful business and professional career.

Many people feel a sense of inner disappointment in their golf games. Flow and creativity feel like lost dreams, while rational thinking and mechanics dominate the thought process. Rational and critical minds are assets needed in certain situations, especially when it comes to solving complex problems. But when playing the game on and off the course, it is hard to analyze what is behind the ball versus where you want the ball to go: the target. Being too rational in our thinking can block our natural creativity and prevent us from achieving our desired outcomes. At the worst, our rational thoughts can lead to critical judgments of ourselves and others. Some of the best players in the world struggle because they get caught up in the process instead of focusing on their target and goals.

Mindfulness and creativity are encouraged through openness and willingness to deal with conflicting ideas that do not have immediate solutions.

We are rarely hit with flashes of brilliance that give us the answers to our problems. For this reason, remaining open to possibilities is instrumental in dealing with our challenges. Adequate coaching will help us understand and reflect on the changes and growth that we achieve. Certainly we don't wish to make mistakes or not perform at our peak performance; however, it is certainly a given that mistakes or not performing at our best will happen in some area of our lives.

There are hundreds of books that teach how to swing a golf club and many thousands of books that attempt to teach how to succeed in business and life. What I have learned from teaching golf, as well as from working with companies for over thirty years, is that the skills necessary for success in golf are exactly the same as those needed to enhance your business and professional career. I believe that true success in any arena is achieved by using a few simple (and yet certainly not always easy) principles. In this book, I will lay out those principles and give you concrete and practical exercises that will help you incorporate them into both your golf game and the game of business. You will find that these concepts will be endlessly beneficial.

To perform well in business or golf, one must understand the basic components of the game. A successful golfer isn't just a person who can hit the ball long. There must also be a thorough knowledge of the technique; the equipment; and the connection to the mind, body, and inner strategy of the game. Once you know those things, you can take corrective measures if something goes wrong. The golfer must understand the course, the strategy, and how to get the most out of his or her ability while dealing with the breakdowns that will inevitably happen and celebrating the successes that will come as well. The same holds true in business and in personal goals.

Perhaps you believe that success comes from hard work and a great deal of practice and determination. But, is this really the whole story? I believe in the value of hard work, but hard work alone doesn't always improve performance. During my time as a professional golf instructor, I saw this every day at the driving range and at the practice tees. People worked for hours on their swings but were never truly focused on the right things and ended the day with very little to show for it. It occurred to me that, while I could teach the mechanics of a good golf swing, coaching people how to think on the golf course required a completely different approach. I began to realize that most of today's golf training is not taught from the basis of the communication between the mind and the body. Instead, the training is mainly mechanical, focusing on grip, stance, and swing.

Over the past many years, my training/coaching seminars and workshops have expanded beyond just golf instruction to working with top business owners and CEOs and their management teams, who, in addition to improving their golf games, are also achieving goals in their careers and businesses. I have worked in a variety of corporate settings: multinational and national companies, Fortune 500 companies, public-sector organizations, manufacturing services, and high-tech industries. In the course of this work, I discovered that releasing individual and organizational creativity involved far more than passing along new skills and techniques and generating new ideas. What was needed was a systematic method customized to individuals to help them focus on their targets, identify and learn to adapt to interference, and evaluate and revise their visions. The material changes come from those willing to challenge the status quo, which may simply mean themselves or the people and organizations in which they can make a difference.

There are more than twenty-seven million golfers in the United States, and, as a PGA golf coach, I can tell you that most of them do not play up to their full potential. People are more concerned about improving their golf swing than they are with improving their golf game. Golfers spend more time learning the mechanics of the swing than they do learning how to focus on a target so that they can end the round with the lowest score.

There are over thirty million small businesses in the United States. As a trainer, coach, and seminar leader, I have seen that the majority of them are not working up to their full potential either. So much time is spent on running a business and managing the day-to-day challenges that the goals of business owners and their teams are lost in the background. The focus of the business can become blurred due to all of the interference that occurs with running a business. Certainly, most people in business want to make more money, just as golfers want to lower their scores. The people who achieve these goals are the ones who have passion and a clear vision, use measurable techniques to reach their targets, and evaluate and correct any interference as it happens. I believe that business owners and leaders, as well as golfers and other athletes, need to be coached on the importance of staying focused through all of life's interference. Current statistics indicate that 85 percent of professional athletes lose a major portion of their income within five years of retiring. This shows that interference can even affect those who seem to be the most focused at what they do at the time, as well as those who seem secure financially. But often, the vision and goals have not been clear long term. This correlation between business and golf issues prompted me to create a business, Performance In Motion.

I grew up around the game of golf with my parents providing the motivation to help me focus on my goals and achieve them. One of my chores was to care for our yard and when I was in ninth grade, I thought of a creative way to get more out of the yard. I envisioned it to be something more than an ordinary backyard and decided to create a putting green instead. I came up with my goals, looked at the total cost of the project, considered how long it was going to take, and most importantly, obtained the buy-in from the rest of my family. My parents loved the idea and agreed to invest in the project.

Focusing on your target while letting go of interference allows for peek performance

I knew that once it was finished I would have to maintain it, but I didn't know just how much work it would be. It taught me to discipline myself because if I didn't water the green or cut it at the right time, it would lead to major problems. Soon the backyard became very popular with our neighbors and became more than just a place to practice. My parents would have parties and host friendly competitions among our friends and family. Without knowing it, I had started on my life's path of helping people create their visions.

I started my career on the links by becoming a golf professional. As I coached successful golfers, I realized that their performance on the golf course was strongly influenced by events off the course and their ability to focus on their game. I also found that how people perform on the links is a reflection of their inner state—including how they feel about themselves and how they think others feel about them.

After many years of coaching golf, I finally decided to put my life's lessons into practice. Just as I had done in ninth grade, I took a vision and made it into a reality. As I continued to see how my approach to coaching in the golf world was helping people improve in other areas of their lives, I began to work with clients who wanted to focus on professional and business issues, not just golf. I set up my own business with an indoor training and coaching studio to provide a nonthreatening, yet challenging place for sales teams, executives, CEOs, business owners, and community leaders to see the possibilities of improved performance using golf and motion as a platform for new possibilities. I have found that when the mind sees what is possible through motion directed at a clear intention/ target, it understands how to make a difference in golf and in business. The most profound improvements come from breakthroughs in thinking and perspective, rather than technical changes.

These methods worked—both on and off the golf course. By the fall of 2005, I had changed the name of my business from Dan DeMuth's Better Golf to Performance In Motion. Whether working with golfers or those who have no interest in the game, I have built a career coaching people and teams to achieve their goals.

In the fall of 2001, the PGA of America recognized my achievements with groups of business executives where I used my coaching techniques to improve their life skills through golf workshops. The workshops provided tools for executives to help them develop changes in mindset, both in the office and on the course.

In 2002, the *Minneapolis Star Tribune* featured an article on the front page of its business section entitled "Golf Whisperer Improving Performance." In the article, my clients acknowledged that much of what they learned through the game of golf also applied to their business and life skills. I was named the 2005 Minnesota PGA Teacher of the Year, and my work has been featured on both radio and television stations, such as WCCO-TV and radio, KARE 11, KSTP 5, Minnesota Business, Twin Cities Business, *Mpls. St. Paul Magazine*, *Tee Times Magazine*, and the *Minnesota Golfer*.

Utilizing the coaching to improve performance in business, personal goals, or golf

The Performance In Motion program has been taught to thousands of people from all walks of life—from CEOs to inner-city youth. The program is effective no matter a person's background, skill level, age, or goals. That is because everyone plays their own game—in golf, business, and personal goals.

Golf is as much a game of the mind as it is a game of skill. The purpose of using the context of golf is that it removes people from the trappings of their existing thought processes. In a completely different setting it is much easier to examine how our thinking affects our performance. When doing golf exercises, people can see that the ball doesn't lie. If they don't focus on a target or they are distracted while swinging the club, the ball is not going to go where they want. Golf works as a metaphor because you can hit a ball with a club even if you have never been on a golf course before. I coach people on their thinking—from finding their target to focusing and then removing any interference that gets in the way of their focus. This experiential learning helps people discover things about themselves and the way they approach situations. Because they can see learning happens through performance, and that learning becomes more real and believable than if I were simply teaching them how to do something.

Most of us do not find it easy to work at this level. At the very least, we have a perception that changing how our minds work is difficult. Developing new skills and techniques is something we approach comfortably, but when it comes to managing our attitudes and beliefs, we find ourselves in unchartered territory. The inner dimensions are harder to handle, simply because they are something you cannot see. Today, with the help of technology, we can now tell what we are thinking and feeling. However, little time has been spent exploring how to actually utilize this knowledge. I call this "believing in what you can't see to produce what you would like to have happen."

Organizations today are taking the inner and creative welfare of their employees very seriously. If top performers and companies are to cope with the challenges ahead, they must find the link between the high demands of professional management and the growing need to manage the inner world of the human being. One of the challenges of changing how we think about our lives and the issues we face is that we get caught up in viewing events and experiences in a fixed way. Sometimes negative experiences color our thinking to the extent that they block us from a mindset of what we should be doing. Learning with a mindset rooted in possibilities versus always trying to fix something can be a breakthrough in itself. When we look for what is possible versus what is wrong, we tend to make changes much faster.

The Performance In Motion program has been honed over many years with the help of many individuals and teams. This book was written as a way of extending the ideas and programs to a wider audience. The exercises and practices talked about here can be done on your own or with your company team. Many of the golf lessons can be done in your own home, backyard, or at your local driving range. All of the business lessons can be done without the use of a professional coach; however, reinforcement is highly recommended to get the most out of your experience. As we will discuss, individual and group coaching is invaluable, but this book will also teach you to become your own best coach.

Although this program uses golf as a medium for teaching the steps to success, part of my aim is to help you achieve your goals as a golfer. The exercises can cut many strokes off your game. However, this is not just another golf instruction manual. Rather, this book is also a compilation of the lessons I have learned about how to apply good golf skills to business and personal goals.

I will incorporate a number of stories from people I have worked with throughout my many years as a PGA golf professional, teacher, and coach. I will also tell you about how these experiential learning lessons changed the way these people did business and how it improved their enjoyment of their personal lives as well as shaved strokes from their golf scores.

Each chapter of the book contains a golf lesson. These lessons are things that anyone can do, whether you are a professional or a novice. Even non-golfers will get a lot out of these lessons as they will aid in achieving other goals. I conduct exercises in a golf setting because golf is a metaphor for reality and what we face in life. You do not need to be a golfer or athlete to change the way you think. Even if you are already a top performer, you will gain new insights to take your game to the next level.

I then relate the golf lesson to businesses and teams and give you an exercise that you can apply in those areas as well. These exercises are designed to help you realize what gets in the way of thinking about issues clearly. They will encourage you to acknowledge preconceptions that may not be accurate and hinder your ability to approach challenges with fresh, artistic eyes. Often, we get locked into one way of thinking and find it difficult to get out of that box. By intentionally practicing new approaches in a variety of motion and other exercises, you are able to examine how you approach situations, free from the everyday issues of work and personal life—and, if you are a golfer, your golf game.

Secrets of the Golf Whisperer is for those people who are interested in developing their creative faculties and managing their world better. It is not just for executives who are struggling to lead their organizations forward in these uncertain times, nor is it just for the golfer or athlete who wants to improve his or her game. It is for those who want a deeper understanding of the process of change and who are looking for new ways to release the creative potential within themselves and their employees. It is for managers and leaders who want to fully understand their staff and who want to create an empowering workplace. It is for people who wish to find another way to work and live, who see that merely rearranging a structure or attending training seminars without follow-up does not tackle the real issues. It is for educators who want to bring deeper meaning to their work. It is also for those concerned about social accountability of organizations.

This book will help you understand how your thoughts affect all aspects of your life. It explores the role of play in the creative process and provides ideas for how to become more open-minded. Upon completion of this book, whether you own your own business, work in a company, want to get better at your golf game, or have a burning desire to achieve something in your life, you will understand how movement, such as golf, can engage both your mind and body to achieve success.

While some people feel personal goals, beliefs, and vision are heavy topics, what follows is not necessarily a heavy discussion. For many of you, this may be the first step to developing a new way of thinking that is essential for successfully navigating your future. Big changes can be made one step or one shot at a time.

Chapter One

Awareness of the Current Situation

Before you can make any changes in your golf games; you're executive, management, or sales teams; your marketing strategies; or any other goal, you need to (or get to) develop clarity and awareness of the current situation. Do you really know what you want out of your experiences? Do you have a clear idea as to why you do what you do what you do? Are you clear about how your business is working and what your actual goals are for developing it or why you do what you do in a business? If you are not achieving your goals, what is holding you back?

Throughout the years many people have come to me for help with their golf games for as many reasons as there are people. I have worked with a total novice whose stated purpose was "not to make a fool of my-self" during the occasional social golf outing. I have also worked with other golf professionals who wanted to shave strokes off their scores or work with their clients to enhance enjoyment and performance. No matter what a person's stated goal is, there is always an underlying reason beneath it. Therefore, before people can change or improve their lives, they need to assess their present situation.

Putting outside the box

Before we talk about self-assessment, I would like to share with you two different exercises that can help you frame the importance of this work. The first exercise is to draw a tree. Give yourself forty seconds to draw a tree. Draw now in the space provided.

The whole point of the exercise is to illustrate how easy it is to miss something because we only focus on what is obvious. When you think of a tree and when you draw it, you typically don't think of the part of the tree that's not visible to you. You simply think of what you can see, not what you can't see, to produce what you would like to achieve. On a smaller scale, this happens at work all the time. For example, a business cuts back on administrative support to save money, but then executives and managers find their time eaten up by admin work, like copying materials, proofing and correcting documents, and who knows what else.

Too often, the obvious thing is to cut staff—it's an obvious cost to the company. But, before doing that, consider the less obvious consequences. Cutting sales staff is like a tree that loses some of its roots. It's less sturdy.

In golf you tend to lose the target when you are in the performance. Thinking about what went wrong with the last shot or what others think about you are just a few of the most common interfering thoughts. Without a clear intent and the awareness of the bigger picture, it can be hard to achieve your peak performance.

Where else might you be missing the roots and/or the things that you can't see to produce what you would like to achieve?

The next exercise has been around for a long time. I really don't know who invented this, but it certainly gets to the point about using your mind to believe and achieve in what isn't always so easy to see. Try connecting four straight lines with a pen or pencil without your pen or pencil leaving the paper to do so.

What were you thinking? Was this hard? Did you know how to do this? How can you relate this exercise to your improvement? Could you follow how you were thinking? Below is one way to achieve what we are talking about.

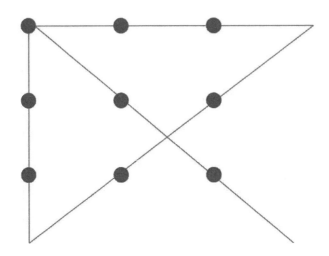

The two exercises relate to how you are thinking and what it takes to look at the possibilities. They require looking beyond what you are used to thinking to achieve extraordinary results.

Self-awareness can be a very difficult thing to discover, which is why I have people fill out a self-assessment form when they take part in our workshops. Shown below is a small example of how we determine the strengths and weaknesses of each individual. Through this form individuals can determine which areas of both business and golf they can improve. There is almost always a correlation between how individuals act in these two areas. For example, those who allow their let downs to get the best of them at work tend to find that this also happens on the course.

Another portion of the self-assessment focuses more on a person's golf game by asking the individual to rate the following aspects of his or her game on a scale of one to nine: driving, fairway woods, fairway irons, approach shots to the green, chipping near the green, pitching, sand play, and putting. While we are primarily trying to determine how good someone is at each of these aspects of the game, it is equally interesting to see how individuals arrive at the numbers. We often find that the perception of the individual is different from the reality of his or her game. For example, perhaps somebody writes down a rating of seven for chipping but solely bases it on how good he or she is in relation to friends. If his or her friends are not any good, then this seven is probably inaccurate. The point is that each person needs to recognize his or her talents in the context of a much bigger picture. This way individuals can work on the things they need to and can avoid wasting their time trying to improve what is already working.

SAMPLE PERFORMANCE PROFILE ASSESSMENT

The assessment and questionnaire on the following pages is designed to be straightforward and to the point. It is designed to help you evaluate yourself and/or your team in order to achieve peak performance. At the end of the assessment, you will be able to interpret the possible conclusions. Performance In Motion will review the data and give you a printout based on how you answered your questions. It is best to review this with others who are coaching you, whether an individual or team.

Name_____Date_____

Compay _____

Title: _____

Improving performance in business and life through the elements of motion

What you want to discover from this experience? _____

_____

What do you believe is restricting you from achieving your business goals? _____

_____

List three operational areas that are causing interference in achieving your business goals. _____

_____

Do you have a five-year strategic plan for your business? _____

_____

Does your business have a clear vision? _____

_____

Do you have annual goals for your team? _____

_____

From one to nine with one being the lowest and nine being the highest, how fully engaged are your team members? _____

_____

From one to nine, how much innovation takes place within your company? _____

Is your team able to effectively communicate internally and externally?

_____

What distinguishes you from your competitors? _____

_____

Golf is the Medium

Do you play golf? Yes No

If yes, why? _____
_____

Current average _____
Target score _____

What do you think is restricting you from achieving your target score?
_____

_____

Would you be interested in learning how to use the strategies and principles of golf to drive your business? _____
_____

shutterstock · 102818663   shutterstock · 141108238

The assessment is to help you become aware of how to get the most out of your experience so you can relate to business, personal goals, golf, sports, fitness, and hobbies.

AWARENESS ASSESSMENT

Circle the number that best describes the statement more often true for you.

If the statement on the left is truer for you, choose a rating toward or on 1.

If the statement on the right is truer for you, choose a rating toward or on 6.

Performance Assessment

1. Distractions often interfere with my performance.		I don't often allow distractions to interfere with my performance.
Business	1 2 3 4 5 6	
Personal Goals	1 2 3 4 5 6	
Golf/Sports/Fitness/Hobby	1 2 3 4 5 6	
2. When I make mistakes, my anger and/or disappointment interfere(s) with my performance.		I still perform and have fun even when I make mistakes.
Business	1 2 3 4 5 6	
Personal Goals	1 2 3 4 5 6	
Golf/Sports/Fitness/Hobby	1 2 3 4 5 6	
3. I sometimes get caught up in the process details and lose sight of my goals.		I maintain focus on my target/goal.
Business	1 2 3 4 5 6	
Personal Goals	1 2 3 4 5 6	
Golf/Sports/Fitness/Hobby	1 2 3 4 5 6	

Business and Team Assessment

1. As a team, you are not willing to make sacrifices (budgets, other team members, etc.) in your department or area of expertise for the good of the team.							As a team, you are willing to make sacrifices in your department or area of expertise for the good of the team.
Business	1	2	3	4	5	6	
2. Team meetings are not productive.							Team meetings are engaging and effective.
Business	1	2	3	4	5	6	

GAP ANALYSIS: ON A SCALE OF 1 TO 9
RATE THE FOLLOWING

Column A:

Rate how important each factor is for you. Choose a rating based upon *how you would like it to be*.

1=low in importance	9=high in importance
A	B

Column B:
Rate how important each factor is for you based on the ACTUAL amount of time and energy you give to it at the present time, i.e. *how it is now*.

Column A: Beliefs		Column B: Reality		
Golf/sports/ fitness/ hobby	Business	Factors	Golf/ sports/ fitness/ hobby	Business
		Joy/Laughter		
		Clear Intention every day		
		My Coaching skills		

EVALUATION: Column A reflects your *beliefs* about business and/or life. Column B reflects your *reality*. If any two parings vary significantly—and you don't like it—you have potential for better performance!

Identify three areas you want to focus on:

1.
2.
3.

No part of the assessment can be reproduced, reprinted, stored in a retrieval system, or transmitted in any form or by any means, electronic, photocopying, recording, or otherwise.

In order to achieve individual greatness or team performance at its best, we must be vulnerable to ourselves and within the team. We must also be respectful to not use others' weaknesses against them (or use our own weaknesses against ourselves). I like to call this *safety and challenge*. If we are too safe and do not show vulnerability, we become "fat and happy" in our ways of thinking and doing. However, too much challenge or vulnerability can scare us and not allow learning to happen within ourselves or our team.

Finding the right combination of safety and challenge is crucial to our development as human beings. An example of a situation with too much safety would be walking an employee along while having him or her complete a task. If there is too much safety, the individual does not ask key questions or discover meaningful answers, so the learning in the situation is very limited. A situation with too much challenge might look like this: the individual is overwhelmed with information and fails to complete the task, later getting yelled at for not doing it correctly. This leads to low self-confidence in the future and does not accomplish anything in the present. It is important to provide the safety before the challenge so the individual or team remains open to the new experience when the challenge is presented.

Successful businesses know where they would like to be and what needs to be done, and they are always looking for ways to improve the process within their own style. When mistakes happen, leaders provide ongoing coaching for employees, which allows employees to learn from their mistakes.

At **Performance In Motion,** we help people define what they want out of a certain experience and achieve it. A question we commonly ask golfers is, "Would you rather be a better ball striker or a better scorer?" These two things are not necessarily the same. Similarly, if you are in business, why do you do what you do? People do not start their own companies because they like the paperwork, e-mails, or phone calls. They start companies for a much larger reason—to help those who need their products or services. Once individuals recognize what is most important to them, the coaching process can begin, and they can find themselves on a clearer path to where they want to be.

When working with people on their golf games, I ask them about their expectations. What do they want to get out of their game? How do they want to improve? I need to get a sense of their frustration. As a coach I find that it isn't simply the mechanics of the game that are holding them back (such as how to hold their club, their stance, their swing, or their lack of openness to directed, desired focus). Something bigger is interfering with their game, and if we don't tackle that issue, the benefit of lessons doesn't always stick. In reality, most people who struggle on the golf course do so because they get so caught up in how they hit the ball and what they look like that they lose sight of the most important thing of all: focusing on the target. My initial questions are designed to get them thinking about the bigger picture—why they are playing golf in the first place. Once we begin to discuss what they are looking for out of the game and how to think about golf in the larger sense, they begin to approach the game with clarity. This is also the same when seeking clarity with other top performers, like CEOs. Many have been great in business but have lost their focus in personal goals. It is easy to focus too much on your business or team and lose sight of yourself.

I met Amy at a workshop I was leading for a group of high-powered business executives. She was one of the top achievers at her company, and her current assessment of her professional life was positive. Still, she had mentioned that her team was not achieving up to her expectations and that her income was not what she desired.

At first glance it would appear that Amy had a lot of clarity about her current situation. After she finished the assessment, though, we discovered that it was not so much her team that she was disappointed in as she was disappointed in herself. She was a perfectionist and was never totally happy with her performance. In this case I advised her to look beyond her current situation. Would a higher income really make her happier? Were there other steps she could take to make her personal life more satisfying?

What are your core values?

Taking an honest assessment about your core values and goals is one of the first steps to making changes happen.

Before you can truly assess where you are in your golf game, personal goals, or business, you get to determine what core values are driving your behavior. If you wish to become clear on your desired outcome, you need to have a set of vital and timeless guiding principles to which you hold yourself accountable. You may have as few as three or more than ten core values that drive your goals. If you are clear on what they are, you will attract like-minded people to your business or to your personal and family structures. This also helps to eliminate the people that simply do not fit into an organization. It is always wise to hire and fire based upon the values of your company. Some examples of core values are listed below:

Treating yourself and others with respect
Striving for greatness
Honesty and integrity
The desire for achievement
Compassion
Enthusiasm, energy, and competition
Accountability
Service to others
Forward thinking
Commitment to learning and growth
Professionalism
Creativity, dreams, and imagination
Having fun
Awareness to details and consistency
Confidence, while being modest and humble
Leadership through teamwork
Thriving on adventure

Safety and challenge, finding the right mix in this order
Empathy

There are, of course, many more values. The above is a small sample to give you an idea of where to start in coming up with your own core values. In my opinion, it is a good idea for executives to have a list of the organization's core values, a list of their own core values, and perhaps require their employees to have a list of core values as well. I also believe all golfers should have a list of their golf core values so that they know what drives them to play. This process of defining your core values and strengths is normally a process that takes some time and one that can certainly change.

Discover the possibilities by playing your own game

However, when dealing with organizations, we should not forget that organizations are, and will always be, composed of people. It is people who make the judgments and decisions that determine the directions and actions of an organization. What we have to look at are the beliefs, attitudes, and core values behind these judgments and decisions to determine why people do what they do.

Here are some examples from the work that I have done with various companies. It is ultimately up to the client, of course, to decide what it is that they want to believe in as their core values:

- Accountability to their team and clients
- Positive culture that is gratifying, rewarding, and respectful
- Treating the customers with respect
- Honesty and integrity for improving the building industry

- Confidence to maintain their pricing while serving the customer with guidelines and accountability

A wealth management team may have the following core values:
- Cutting-edge knowledge
- Integrity and trustworthiness
- Client needs first
- Extraordinary service
- Trustworthiness

A golfer may have the following core values:
- Learning about self and others
- Competitive with and respectful to others
- Commitment to each shot
- Self-belief
- Openness to coaching when needed
- Having fun
- Enjoying the company of others
- Love of nature
- Permission to win, given by self

It doesn't take much for us to get off track when we are living our busy lives. Whether in business or in golf, we can easily get distracted by interference—either internal or external. Our job as leaders is to establish our core focus and not let anything distract us from our target. It is important to remind ourselves of the core focus at all times because it is easy to get bored. In golf I have seen many great players go by the wayside simply because they lost their target and started searching for the perfect swing.

You DO have core values about your golf game, your life, and your business. Take the time to make a list of what they are, and then check it periodically to determine if those values have grown or changed and if your behavior is in line with your values. For example, if one of your core values is "family comes first" and yet you find yourself neglecting your family for your business, you are not truly in sync with what is important to you.

Once people have determined their core values, I ask them to assess their strengths and what interferes with achieving their goals. Take a few minutes and fill out this scorecard for yourself.

Strengths

List at least three of your strengths and describe examples that demonstrate your proficiency. This is a valuable exercise to share with your team or others close to you.

Strength	Evidence from work	Evidence from life	Evidence from sport or hobby

Next, examine your scorecard of strengths and list the item(s) that seem to interfere most in keeping you from using these strengths to act upon your goals and plans. Finally, list some strategies you can take to help you manage the anxiety, face the fear, and overcome the obstacles that keep you from acting on your plan.

You will notice that I don't have you make a list of your weaknesses. Instead, I have you focus on what interferes with your strengths. Focusing on perceived weaknesses only increases them. What you focus on in life tends to increase. What you focus on in golf becomes your target. (Have you ever noticed how often your ball goes straight to that water hazard you can't seem to help focusing upon?)

Noticing interference allows you to develop strategies for managing it. We will be discussing interference and ways to manage and avoid it later in this book. For now, think of things that cause you interference (perhaps a constantly ringing phone, other people on the golf course, or a spouse's criticism) and then think of ways to manage that interference (turning off the ringer on your phone, etc.).

	Interference	What is causing it?	Strategy for managing interference
Work Personal goals Sport/Hobby			

Current Situation—Personal Responsibility

It is hard to improve your golf game, your sales figures, your company's profitability, or anything else for that matter until you have taken an honest look at where you are right now. This means becoming aware of how you can make a difference. What are you really shooting in the game of golf? With all the mulligans, gimmes, etc., people think they keep score, but do they really?

How many sales do you actually close? What income do you actually take home from your business? This is not what you hope to do or project you will do but the actual figure.

When I ask golfers to tell me what they score, I usually find that they either cannot answer or are in complete denial of their score. They often make it better because they do not count each stroke, sometimes because they have low esteem for their game. When I work with companies, I often find that they talk gross (rather than net) sales and sometimes have very little idea of their actual profitability (or lack thereof).

Don came in for help with his golf game because he had, as he called it, "a wicked slice." While he knew that his drives seldom went straight down the fairway, he really had no idea of what he scored, since he routinely took a drop on almost every hole. He laughed as he told me he lost about five balls per round but never counted lost balls as an extra stroke. It may be fine in some cases to not keep score in golf, but in business we do not have that choice.

Don had recently left a position as a junior associate in a large law office and had started his own practice. I asked him how the practice was doing, and it soon became clear to me that Don had no more idea of his bottom line in law than he did in golf. He told me that he took a $5,000 draw each month to support himself. His law practice wasn't functioning in the black yet, he said, so he was drawing against a line of credit to meet his living expenses. Don did not seem to see that, in both his golf and his business, he was being dishonest with himself and not aware of the actual situation.

In order to change anything, you need to know where you are starting from. In my program, I have people fill out a list of their strengths, as you have seen. This list will apply to your golf, your business, and other areas of your life. A person who is persistent, for example, will apply that character trait to all areas of his or her life. We often tend to focus on our weaknesses instead of on our strengths, so I ask people to list at least three of their strengths and give evidence of how that strength shows itself in work, personal goals, and golf (or another sport or hobby).

DEVELOPING YOUR GOALS

Once you have assessed your current situation, core values, strengths, and interfering factors, you should then take a look at your goals. Millions of words have been written about goals. Everyone tends to set goals, yet it is estimated that less than 4 percent of people ever achieve their goals. Why? I believe it is because our intentions are not always clearly stated or understood, or they have an emotional buy-in. We really don't know what our goals are and thus have no way to know if we achieve them. For example, many people have the goal of "making more money." Since there is no way to measure what "more" means to them, they often feel that they have not achieved this goal, no matter how much they make.

I have discovered over my years of doing this work that people think they have a clear goal but can't articulate it clearly. If you don't write down your goals, they tend to be forgotten, misplaced, or ignored. Once people do write them down, the goals become clearer, more focused, and measurable. Telling other people about your goals makes them become real to you and creates accountability. After all, you have spoken them out loud and given them power by doing so. There is nothing new about written goals. However, attaching the goals to experiential learning is new. This experience becomes long-lasting when you achieve something that you set out to do and start believing in what you can achieve in the future.

A goal has an objective and a purpose. It is far more than a dream or a wish. It is a dream that has been committed to being acted upon. Goals need to be stated clearly and to be measurable. In golf your score is measurable, while your enjoyment of the game is much harder to measure. In business, your profit is measurable, whereas your friendships in the workplace are more difficult to assess. Still, you have the ability to measure if you are finding enjoyment in both places. For many years I would hear how golfers could score low on one nine but not keep it together for the whole round. They would explain that they would get nervous as they were scoring low. This simply explains that people never practiced going low before they got in this experience. And even worse when they did shoot their career round, they would verify it by saying how unbelievable that was to achieve—only to later make it unbelievable in future rounds.

In life, your goals are your target, just as the hole is your target in golf. There can be no coaching if there is no target or goal. Without goals, individuals just wander through life aimlessly, stumbling along without knowing where they are going or how they are doing. In golf we need to set a goal in order to measure our progress. We need to keep score and can do so by defining our own games before we start to play.

You may have observed that the lives of highly successful people are integrated around a purpose. Surrendering to the goals that you would like to achieve is an art in and of itself.

On occasion, all of us have woken up on a weekend day with no plans, no agenda (either mental or written), and no real purpose for that day. While we all enjoy a day with no plans on occasion, we do tend to drift through the day without clarity, often not feeling good about ourselves for what we have done. This is not to say that you shouldn't enjoy your weekends with family and friends maybe just simply sitting by the pool or beach or reading a book. However, most of us get bored with those kinds of days quickly. Being committed to a goal and achieving it can be much more enjoyable than relaxation.

It is important that your goals are precise and that they hold you accountable. Too many people get stuck in their golf games and in their businesses because they become comfortable in their old ways of doing things and are unwilling to change.

I have observed that the structure of most small businesses is very loose or nonexistent. Similarly, time and time again, I have watched golfers fall back into their same patterns simply because they have no concrete goals for getting better.

You will learn how to use the accountability scorecards to so that you don't fall into this trap. This will enable you to implement a structure that encourages expansion and clearly defines the roles and responsibilities in your business. In golf you will use the scorecards to further help you refine your game and give yourself permission to achieve your goals.

PUT GOALS IN WRITING

The first step in goal-setting is getting a realistic picture of where you are now. It is like following a map. You have to know where you are now in order to map out where you are going. In golf many people don't really know what they score. Amateur golfers tend to be "creative" in their scoring, often ignoring their mulligans, using a lot of "gimmes" while putting, and changing their lie when it is too difficult. I have nothing against this type of scoring, but for the purpose of mapping your goals, you do need to know what you actually score when you count all your shots. If you choose to play the game of golf without keeping score, which for many might be the right choice, you should first develop some other measurable system to determine your performance.

The same thing is true for many of the small businesses with which I have worked. Their accounting practices can be so vague that they are not completely sure if they are profitable or not.

Over ten thousand people have been through my workshops or seminars on site. Most of them came to me believing they had clear goals "in their heads" on what they wanted to achieve. However, when I asked them to write down these goals, they were unable to articulate them clearly. Without clear, specific, and written goals, people tend to end up somewhere other than where they want to be.

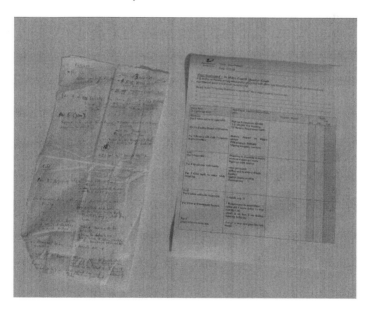

Many great ideas have emerged from scribbled notes like those on this napkin. On the right is a more systemized method of measuring goal progress.

The other reason it is important to write down goals, especially for those in my company seminars, is that it helps employees and management to know what is important to the company and to the other individuals on their team. Trying to fit into how others see you can be a big problem. While CEOs and business owners may know what the company goals are, their employees may not. Writing down goals helps owners and employees start working toward the same goals to benefit each other. Employees start seeing their job as more than simply earning a paycheck, while employers and owners often get a new appreciation for the value of each of their unique employees. After all, if the company does well, the employees benefit (and vice versa).

In my program, I have people write down their goals and help them redefine them through the SMART goals guidelines. Use these guidelines as a way to set your own goals, whether for your golf game, business, or personal goals.

SMART GOALS HAVE THE FOLLOWING CHARACTERISTICS:

SPECIFIC

Be specific about what, how, and why. Use action verbs to describe what you are going to do. Examples of some verbs you can use include

- Reduce
- Compile
- Lead
- Coordinate
- Organize
- Develop

Describe what you want to accomplish and why it is important. Explain how you are going to do it.

MEASURABLE

If you can't measure it, you can't demonstrate you have achieved your goal. Be specific. Describe success in terms that show progress. For example: hire three new people in two months, reduce inventory by 30 percent within six months, sign four new accounts worth a total of $25K in three months, average no more than two putts per hole, reduce my score by five points in two months, etc.

Build in short-term measurements if it makes it easier to track progress. Make sure you establish concrete criteria that can be measured. The more objective the goal, the greater the likelihood you will achieve it.

ATTAINABLE

Choose goals that are within your ability to achieve. Make sure you have the resources, skills, ability, and attitude, plus the financial support you need. You want to stretch, but if the goal is beyond your reach, you are likely to fail. If you are currently shooting over one hundred, don't aim for the seventies in a month.

REALISTIC

Is the goal something you have the capability to make happen? Your goal should push you, but it should also be something that you have the skills to accomplish. It should fit within the needs of your organization. In your personal life, it should be something you can achieve in light of other realities. Make sure your goals require effort on your part but aren't so difficult that you are doomed from the beginning.

TIMELY

Establishing a deadline for your goals gives you a clear target for tracking progress. Without a timeline, you don't have a sense of urgency, and the goal will never become the priority it needs to be.

(Though out the book you will read different success stories identified by this image.)

Below is an e-mail I received several years ago from a past client of mine, Scott. He had attended the program right after he had graduated from college. In fact, Scott and I met when I was teaching a business, life, and golf program at the University of Minnesota. Scott took my program because he wanted to work on his golf game and also wanted to clarify his goals and vision on the business he was forming. This is his story:

Dan,

Quite the trip. As I mentioned at our last get-together, I planned on spending some time in Phoenix visiting my brother and playing some golf. I almost decided at the last minute not to take the clubs because they would be a pain to lug around. I am glad I did, though.

Neither my dad (he went to Arizona with me) nor my brother golf, so I went out yesterday (Wednesday) alone and was paired up with a couple of retirees at this course in Phoenix. The front nine went well. I ended up with 4 bogeys for a 40. I was hoping to nail a putt on Hole 9 to get my 39, but just left it high.

The back nine started off kind of rough—a triple bogey on a par 5, a few three putts, and a double bogey. Though I was not focused on the outcome (ha, ha) as I approached the 18th hole, I knew I needed a par on the 359 yard, par 4, to get an 85. This would be a personal best for me, well within reach.

The gentleman I was playing with, who was a regular at the course, suggested that with my distance I should go ahead and drive one out over a bunker to get closer to the green. With a pretty stiff breeze at my back, I decided to just hammer one out toward the green (to the left and behind the bunker) and see what happened.

I nailed it right on line, it bounced a couple of times in the rough, kicked over a ridge in front of the green, and disappeared somewhere onto the green. Unfortunately, the foursome in front of us was still putting out. Obviously, I was quite embarrassed that I hit into them and waved my arms and club in the air to signal my apology. They enthusiastically waved backed and were jumping around a bit, so I figured it must have been pretty close.

My partner drove his cart over to his ball, and I raced up to the green in my cart to apologize in person to the group ahead. When I got there, one of the guys started walking toward me and said, "We'll let you come up and grab the ball out of the cup yourself."

Obviously I thought it was a joke and laughed a bit, but he was serious—hole in one! I grabbed the ball out of the cup, shook hands with the group, apologized for my poor etiquette, offered them a drink (they declined), and headed back to watch my partner finish up the hole.

So I ended up with an 82. Hit my scoring goal for the year in March in a slightly nontraditional way, but what the heck.

Scott

Scott had achieved his goal of shooting an eighty-two within three months of beginning the program and setting the goal. The uniqueness of his reaching his goal was his approach to the course (and, of course, the hole in one). On the golf course, he had a breakdown on his back nine, but he didn't give up. He stayed the course, learned how to deal with his letdowns, and had a major breakthrough on the eighteenth hole. Not only was this a hole in one on a par four, he scored his goal with the end in mind. He achieved his goal of shooting an eighty-two. The game of golf demonstrated to him how he could overcome ups and downs, conquer interference, and remain focused on his goal. Accomplishing this was a great help to Scott, which he would later bring back to his business goals.

PERFORMANCE
IN MOTION

The Assessment

Mastery Personal Profile

Date _1-6-06_

Name _Scott_   Company ▮▮▮▮

Address ▮▮▮▮

City ▮▮▮▮   State ▮ Zip ▮   Birthdate ▮▮▮

Home Phone ▮▮▮   Work Phone ▮▮▮

Cell Phone ▮▮▮   E-mail ▮▮▮

Do you play golf? _x_ Yes _____ No. If yes, have you taken lessons before? _____ Yes _x_ No.

If yes, what part of your game have you worked on? _____

What was the outcome of these lessons? _____

_____

Number of Rounds played per year _20-25_ Current average score _92_ Target score _82_

What do you want to get out of this experience? _Improve my golf game + focus on/for course_

What do you think is restricting you from achieving your target score? _Blow up_

holes, compounding frustration at times

Have your clubs been fitted for you? _Y_ Who do you play golf with? _Friends/Co-workers_

Why do you play golf? _Fun + challenge, get outside_

Peak Experience – Think about a time (work, sports, hobbies, home. etc.) when you were operating at "peak performance" (everything seemed to be in synch). What caused you to perform in this manner? _Seeing the target and connecting_

with it (86 round in 03)

Circle the number that best describes what you are thinking about or focusing on most often when you are on the course, in relation to the following attributes: Also, consider these questions in relation to your Life and Business. Use the following symbols to represent life, business, and golf: Life= □; Business= Δ; Golf = O

1. I focus on keeping score	1	②Δ	3	4	5	6	I play unattached to the score
2. I approach the game seriously	Δ1	2 O3	4	5	6	I focus on having fund when I'm playing
3. As I'm playing, I concentrate on Mechanics	1	2	3 □Δ	⑤	6	As I'm playing, I focus on the target
4. When I play, I want to look good	1	2	3 □Δ	⑤	6	When I play, I want to feel good
5. As I play, I think about the outcomes of my shots	1	2	3 □O	5	6	As I play, I think about creating possibilities
6. Time between my shots is focused on the next shot	1 Δ2	□3 O4	5	6	Time between my shots is spent enjoying the course and surroundings
7. As I play the game, I think about perfection	1	2	3 ΔO4	⑤	6	As I play the game, I keep a sense of playfulness
8. I think a lot about my bad shots	1	2	3 □4 ΔO5	6	I think a lot about my good shots

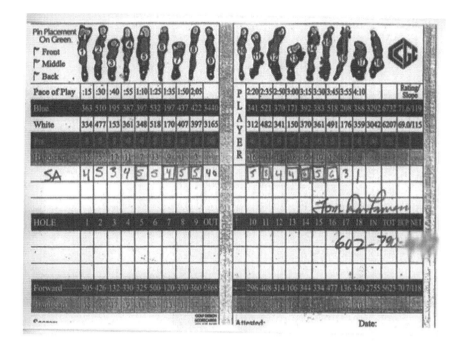

This was Scott's scorecard from that day. He reached his goals within three months and on his first round of the year. The signature was the guy who he was playing with. He wrote down his phone number so that in case people didn't believe Scott, they could call him and he would confirm.

Scott's double eagle hole-in-one on the last hole to achieve his goal of 82 is a constant reminder to him of the importance of writing down goals to know what it is you want to accomplish in life (what we call "clarifying the vision"). As he saw future successes on his scorecard, he began to believe he could accomplish other goals as well, whether it was in business, life, or recreation. Writing down and working toward his goals gave Scott the confidence to ultimately start his own successful business.

SET A TIMETABLE, BUT BE ADAPTABLE

A person determined to achieve maximum success learns that progress is made one step at a time. Even though the goals that we set in my program are based on a monthly and quarterly basis, that doesn't mean that all the goals will be achieved within that timetable. Some of the goals may need to be tracked by the hour, while the others are the result of how we manage our overall days, weeks, and months. In some cases, an hour may be easy, but forever maybe difficult.

Sometimes it appears that someone achieves success all at once. But if you check the past history of the people who seemed to arrive at the top suddenly, you'll discover a lot of groundwork was previously laid to achieve these goals. As one of my highly successful clients once told me, "When I first started my business, I waited for my one big break. What I have learned is that there really isn't a 'one big break.' There are a series of small breaks."

When writing our goals, it is important to remind ourselves of a couple of main strategies take into account to improve the quality of our lives. One strategy is to allow external conditions that are realistic to match our goals. The other strategy is to change how we experience external conditions and work within our goals better. These strategies can't seem to work alone by themselves. When we change external conditions might seem to work at the beginning, but if a person is not in control of his or her thought/consciousness, the fear of the past can take over and previous anxieties can set into place.

The next time you see a particularly poised, clear-thinking, effective person remind yourself that he or she was not born that way. A lot of conscious effort, invested day by day, made the person who he or she is. Building new habits while destroying old ones is a day-to-day process.

When we discuss setting goals, someone always comments about how things happen to distract him or her from achieving goals. There are, of course, many factors that are outside our control in our lives. Part of life is dealing with obstacles and interference. When we run into construction on the road, for example, we don't usually have to go all the way back to our starting destination. We remap our trip and take another route from where we are. It is rare that a person who has achieved a high level of success has not had to take a few detours. We don't have to change our goals; we just have to travel a different route to achieve them.

TRACKING GOALS

After you have set your goals, it is necessary to track them. Otherwise, you will not be able to tell what is working and what is not. In golf we call this the handicap, which is a measure for how the golfer is doing. In business, you might call it a quarterly report or even a tax statement. Measurement is an integral part of everything you wish to achieve.

Several years ago, a former client of Performance In Motion helped me design a scorecard on which we could track our goals in business, life, and golf/sport/hobby. The scorecard helps us determine if we are not only achieving our goals but also if we are having fun along the way.

KEEPING A SCORECARD

After creating your overall life goals, it is helpful to look at what it is that you wish to have happen both in the short term and long term. For the purposes of my training, I call short-term goals those that are in the imme. diate future, with long-term goals being anything ninety days and beyond. Usually the short-term items are things that need to be accomplished to create your longer-term goals.

When you make a long-term goal, it is not easy to see the steps you need to take to achieve it. But, when you break it into shorter-term goals, you create a map to take you where you wish to go. In business, you need to know where your organization is headed and how you expect it to get there. I demonstrate this concept in golf by suggesting to people that they play a hole backward. I have actually done this on a golf course (with permission from the course). You can also do it in your mind's eye, though, imagining yourself teeing off from the green and taking shots backward toward the tee box. To play a hole backward in golf, we start at the hole and work our way back to the tee box, thus seeing the hole from a completely different perspective. In business or life, you can start with your goal in the far future and then work your way back to the present.

For the purpose of this exercise, imagine yourself happy and successful ten years from today.

BUSINESS

- What kind of work are you doing?
- What is your income level?
- How much authority do you have?
- What level of responsibility do you seek?
- What honors have you achieved?

GOLF/SPORT/HOBBY

- What have you achieved? (scores, handicap, awards)
- What has changed about the way you are playing?
- At what level are you playing?
- What is the enjoyment level of your game?

Now, fill in the scorecard below with concrete and measurable things you can do in the next ninety days that will aid in bringing those larger goals into being. These goals are reevaluated every quarter of a year and should be organized accordingly. The par-three goals should be short-term goals that may not be very difficult to achieve. Par-four goals are bigger goals that might not be attainable in the very near future but are still relatively short-term. Par-five goals are longer-term goals that may take multiple months to achieve. The decision about actual length of time it takes to achieve each goal will vary depending on the individual or team.

YOUR SCORECARD – NINE HOLES: FIRST QUARTER GOALS

Fill in this scorecard setting measurable goals that will allow you to realize the professional and recreational gains you intend on achieving.

List three areas you want to work on:

1. _____

2. _____

3. _____

Focus Area (2-5 goals per area)	Action steps I need to take to reach goals.	Progress / Results	Not Fun	Score OK	Fun
Business: Par 3 Par 4 Par 5					
Personal goals: Par 3 Par 4 Par 5					
Sport/Hobby/Golf: Par 3 Par 4 Par 5					

On the golf course, a round of golf is really achieved one shot at a time. In business, success can be measured by the achievement of many small steps that can create big changes in a very short period of time.

I have seen golfers go from shooting in the one hundreds to the low to mid seventies within six months, all by taking one shot at a time.

Using the above form as a guide, fill in the focus area with two to five goals you can achieve in the next ninety days. For each goal, make concrete action steps on how you can achieve these goals, and then, over the course of the next ninety days, make notes as to your progress and results. In my roundtable groups, we use this method to help one another become aware of our accomplishments or areas in which we need to put more focus. We also keep track of our enjoyment level by reporting it with a check mark on green (fun), yellow (OK) or red (not fun).

At the end of each quarter, the clients give themselves a number that correlates to par in golf. So, a client might have a goal of selling ten products by the end of a month. An action step to achieve this goal might be to reach out to one hundred prospects. While the client may have achieved the goal of selling ten products, he or she may put a check mark in the yellow column since it was not that much fun. By being aware of whether they are achieving goals and how much they are enjoying it, clients can begin to determine what is holding them back from checking the green column.

The overall intent of filling out this scorecard is to have fun while remaining focused on our goals. While building positive day-to-day habits and changing old, negative ones is a process in and of itself, we can have fun while we achieve our goals.

Of course, life is sure to give us interference, and it is important to take detours in stride. There are many factors outside of our control that affect our progress and goals, just as the game of golf is affected by weather issues, course hazards, and other players. It is rare to meet a person who has achieved a high level of success and has not had to take detours on the road to that success.

The progressive business knows that how strong it will be in the future depends not on what it does in the future but rather on what it does this year. Likewise, the championship golfer knows that each hole is played one stroke at a time.

Chapter Two

Discovering the Possibilities

W hy is it that so many people play their best golf in the very beginning or end of the season? I have witnessed for myself and many other clients that the mindset is totally open to the possibilities at those times. The state of mind is unattached to the outcome but clear on the intention. Target, focus, relax, and release. Certainly the mind isn't bogged down with the grip, stance, and swing of the game. Rather, the mind and body are open to play and excited to be there. Most people know what this energy feels like but can't describe it. The mind is open with a clear focus on the target, and the heart is engaged by relaxation and deep breathing. The golfer shows true passion and love of the game in the moment and is excited to hit the shot.

After you have made a full assessment of your current situation and set your goals, you are then (and only then) ready to discover the possibilities for changing your game / your life. It is, after all, impossible to successfully change things until you see them clearly and have set goals for what you wish to change. Once you are aware of the current situation, it is then time to see the myriad of possibilities to change, improve, or even accept. In Chapter 1 you not only learned how to assess your present situation but also how to set your goals. Now, we will take you beyond that to your visions and possibilities.

WHAT IS YOUR VISION?

Making and achieving goals is really about focusing on the short term (you notice even the "long-term" goals on the scorecard are ninety-day goals). While setting goals is very important, you also need to ask yourself if you are living your dream. Is your life today everything you thought it would be? You need to have a vision of your life as well as clear goals.

 Joel and I were competitors on different high school golf teams. Through our meetings on the golf course and our love for the game, we became friends. Before Joel was about to graduate, I asked him about his future plans. "I'm moving out to New York to be an actor and a model," he said. I remember thinking it was an interesting dream—I didn't laugh, and I wasn't shocked, but I was impressed with his vision of his life.

Joel and I lost contact, and I didn't see him again for about twenty years. Then, one day, I was watching the premiere of the movie *The Legend of Bagger Vance* and saw him in the movie theater, up on the movie screen. He was playing the role of the golfer Bobby Jones, with Will Smith playing Bagger Vance. It was a fitting place for me to see him out on the golf course again. Joel had made it. I was struck once again by the power of a vision.

A vision goes beyond dreams and goals. It goes to the very core of who you are and who you want to be. Joel's high school vision became his adult reality in part because his vision of his future was crystal clear. What does it look like when you are open to the possibilities? What is your vision?

I find that when I work with leadership teams there is a good chance each person's vision differs from others on the team. This is because the owner of the business has not clearly defined his or her vision for the company or has changed it without telling the employees. It is important that everyone on the team not only be able to understand the vision for the company but also be able to clearly articulate it. It is very difficult to believe or achieve high performance without clarity of vision. In my experience of playing on several teams, we won because we had a vision, and lost when we either didn't have one or didn't stick to it.

I also have had the opportunity to work with many entrepreneurs over the years, and most of them can clearly see their own visions; the problem is that they think that everyone else in their company can see the vision too. However, in many cases employees don't. As a result, great visions are left unrealized, staff members end up confused, and leaders end up frustrated. By clarifying your vision, you will make better decisions about the people around you, the processes, finances, strategies, and customers. Without a clear vision, doubt, confusion, and interference set in. Owners or CEOs of companies must take their visions out of their own heads and clarify them to all members of the company.

In order to do this in my coaching program, we help our clients create a vision board. A vision board is a technique for turning your vision into a concrete reality, and it can be very useful and effective if taken seriously and done with purpose. I started creating my own vision boards in 2002 when a golf client and friend of mine introduced me to the process. Since then, I have made a point to do one every year. It is amazing how powerful the mental images become when they are part of who you are. I highly recommend creating one.

While having a coach and program is very useful, often because we force you to do things you would otherwise not do, you can always go through this process on your own, creating and clarifying your vision and then sharing it with family and friends. Speaking your vision out loud makes it real and concrete. It changes it from being a dream to being a practical vision that can be embraced and acted upon.

By now, if you are following the suggestions in this book, you have identified your core values, created short-term and longer-term goals, and recognized your strengths and the things that are interfering with your goals. The next step is to put these things into a clear vision of your game and life. In my experience, the best and most visual way to do that is to create a vision board. It is helpful for others to see how you describe your vision when relating to the mental images.

CREATING A VISION BOARD

A vision is about where we want to be someday. It is not about how we get there. That's why images are so much more powerful than words. Visioning is a right-brain activity that frees us from the usual constraints of our left-brained, analytical mind. Goals are set with our left brain. Visions are created with our right. Images give us a way to visualize what we want to achieve without letting words get in the way.

In my programs we create vision boards to free up thinking, creating a vision using images instead of words. Words are important, but they tend to be concrete, while images are about possibilities. The first step in creating the vision board is to let go of conscious control of what goes on it. You get to allow your mind to see things from a larger and different perspective.

I ask people to find images that appeal to them or that they find interesting in magazines, online, and in other places. It is not just about identifying images that match their goals, but rather finding images that make their hearts sing. Often, these photographs and drawings will reveal your unconscious wishes or desires, some of which you may not even be aware.

One reason we do the vision board after we do our goals is to see if our goals are actually in line with our vision. I have found it interesting to do it this way so that people do not "force" their goals to fit their vision but instead to see how the two complement each other.

In many cases, inspiration comes to us in images rather than words. When Einstein discovered the nature of light, he was not sitting at his desk solving equations. He was sitting on a grassy hillside, looking up at the sun through half-closed eyelids, imagining the light beam traveling from the sun to his eye. His inspiration occurred through an image, but it occurred after many years of mental preparation and reflection.

It helps if you ask yourself these five questions before searching for your images:

- What do I really want to achieve?
- Why am I doing what I am doing?
- What is the most important thing to me?
- What are my dreams for business, personal goals, golf, sports, and other hobbies?
- If I only had five years to live, does this matter?

I ask my clients to sleep on their image boards (not literally, of course, but to ask their subconscious to give them images in their dreams). Sleep is one of the best incubators for visions. During sleep the activity of the conscious, rational mind is at its lowest. Not only does our unconscious speak to us in our dreams, but we may wake up with new perspectives on a task. From time to time, we may find ourselves dreaming about a problem in our life, and our dreams may teach us about certain aspects of the situation we did not see before.

After people have found images that appeal to them, speak to them, and make them happy, they are instructed to paste these images on a sheet of poster board or on a picture frame. Some vision boards are very elaborate with borders and phrases and pictures neatly and artistically placed. Other boards look a little thrown together. How the board looks only matters to the individual, though. What is important is the care and thought that were put into the content of the images. If you slap together a few images that you just "sort of" like, your vision will lack clarity and not feel true to you.

One thing that surprises many people is that their vision may be very different from the goals they have set for themselves. For example, your goal may be to create a successful business, making X amount of dollars. But all the images on your vision board are of relaxation and fun. This is not a problem. It simply means that your goals or vision might need to be altered in some fashion. Can you think of a way in which you can make your business more relaxing and fun? Can you figure out how to live abundantly on less money so that you have more free time? What are the possibilities? Can you believe in them?

After their vision boards are created, I suggest to people that they then share the board with others, putting their visions into words. In my program we share our vision boards at a roundtable. Each person shows their board and then describes the images and what they mean to them. If you don't have a roundtable, be brave enough to share your vision board with your spouse, coworkers, or a close friend. However, it is also important to share your vision with people who are trained to give nonjudgmental feedback, be supportive, and ask key questions. Words clarify and solidify your visions. Pictures help you see your vision. Words help you put that vision into motion.

My niece, Briana, created a vision board and then shared it with a group of others who were in the program one year. A particularly interesting image she had found for her board was a picture of a golf ball cut in half. Briana had played golf for many years but never knew what the inside of a golf ball looked like. As she discussed this with the group, she realized that this resembled some of her relationships in

that no matter how well she thought she knew a person, she did not know what was going on in the inside them. Her image was powerful to her and reminded her that there is much more that goes on with people than what you can see. Her vision was to have clarity and understanding, not only in golf, but also in relationships by learning about people through their actions, not just their words.

Similarly, on my own vision board one year, I had found a picture of an iceberg. In this case, the iceberg was shown both above the water and below the water. Underneath the water, it was about ten times the size it was above. This goes to show that we only get a glimpse of certain situations, when, in reality, they might be much larger or more complicated than they initially seem.

Creating a vision board allows you to bring your vision from your head to paper. It allows for you to believe in yourself. As you go through this process, it is important to share it with others whether it is in your organization (for business visions), your family and friends, or your team (for golf). By getting everyone on the same page, you will find that problems get solved more quickly.

Explaining the vision allows for clarity to get your thoughts out of your head, to learn from others, to be challenged, and to further believe in your vision.

Creating a vision board is designed to give you clarity on what you want to achieve without being perfect. The mental images that you are seeking to attract can simply relate to what it is that you would like to have happen for yourself. This will help you clearly define what it is that you want to achieve, even when others may not understand until you explain it to them. It is your vision board, and it is not always necessary to get approval from outside sources. Still, describing your vision board to others puts clarity in your mind. It is not necessary for them to approve or understand, but it is necessary that you hear your own voice telling of your vision.

Keep your vision board after it is created and continue to look at these images until they become part of your subconscious. Some of my clients have framed their boards and display them in a prominent place in their homes and offices. Others keep them in a closet and look at them when they get dressed. The more you see your images, the more you become who you already are. When you focus sharply on your vision board, it helps to override interference, whether from distractive thoughts, negative ideas, fear and doubt, or other people's perspectives that may otherwise penetrate your subconscious. The vision board engrains what you desire into your consciousness and attracts what you want through visual repetition, a fixed goal, and a clear picture of the desire. The goal of the vision board is to transform what is in the subconscious into reality. I must warn you that what you put on the vision board must be used to help you achieve your desired outcomes and not be used harmfully against others. It should also have positive images that you want to attract or achieve that are rightfully yours to achieve.

Joe was an attorney at a company in Minnesota that was being bought out by another company that was deciding to move their headquarters to Indiana. He was in my roundtable group at the time working on his golf, business, and personal goals. Joe was struggling with his performance on the course, which it didn't make sense as he hit the ball very well during the program. One day we had a follow-up phone session.

I asked Joe to meet me at my studio and to bring his vision board with him. Joe took the vision work lightly. He had put together his vision on the inside of a grocery bag. One picture had explained it all—it was a guy that looked like him writing with his head collapsed on a desk. To me, it was a vision of the breakdown Joe was experiencing in both in business and in golf.

I asked Joe why he wanted to attract that image into his life and game. He couldn't really answer, except when he put the vision board together, he said the picture reminded him of himself. I told him that was in the past and asked, "What do you want to do now to make a difference for yourself?" Joe took the image off his vision board, and we burned it in the studio. At the same time, I was able to ask him some key questions that allowed for him to leave the studio and talk to the CEO of the company that he was working for at the time.

Joe had to take the risk and learn the truth. By asking the CEO some questions, he did learn the truth, but initially it was not what he wanted to learn. He discovered that the company was moving out of state. Joe asked if they would be willing to allow him to work remotely, but they declined. However, the company was willing to give him a year's severance pay to get some work done (about a month's worth), and that allowed Joe to get his work done and network within the community to explore his options with clarity. Within a few months, Joe ended up being the head of counsel with an insurance company.

The breakthrough for Joe was the decision to ask the key questions that would allow him to realize what he could do to make a difference for himself and others. Joe's direct interference with his golf game was about his business. The tensions surrounding his job completely affected his mindset on the course.

There likely will be many phases to your vision board. It grows as you grow. You may find yourself adding, removing, and changing images as your goals become clearer. You may need to make a new vision board, as your dreams and goals at age fifty will likely be very different than they were at age twenty. We will discuss updating your vision board in a later chapter.

ASSESSING THE POSSIBILITIES: THE PUTTING EXERCISE

 John came to me because he "just couldn't sink a putt anymore," as he put it. After assessing his situation and watching him putt, we both realized John was so stressed about putting that his shoulder became stiff and his swing rigid. John not only needed to see himself playing the game differently through video, but he also needed to learn new possibilities of ways to putt. As I do with all my clients, I encouraged John to see the possibilities of different ways of putting by doing the following exercise.

The putting exercise is one of the exercises we do early in my training program. A wide variety of people have done this exercise, from golfers to sports teams to companies. It can be used by everyone to demonstrate how possibilities they may never have considered often turn out to be the best options for them. From this experience, people learn that the ball doesn't lie and that changes might be necessary in order to see improvement. In John's case he was able to perform way better with his eyes closed. It had helped him focus on the target and let go of the interference.

Discovering the possibilities using the putting exercise

You can do this exercise at home, in the office, on the practice green, or at a nearby golf course. It can be done alone or with a partner and should take less than ten to fifteen minutes to complete. You will need a putter, a golf ball (three balls work best), and a golf hole. If you're doing this at home or in the office, you can simply cut a hole in the middle of a paper plate and turn it upside down on the floor. For those of you wondering, a regulation golf hole is four and one-quarter inches in diameter.

Set the golf balls at approximately three feet, six feet, and nine feet from the hole (assume a good stride is about three feet). You'll be putting three times from each distance using a different approach after each nine putts. You will keep score by filling in the chart below.

Only hit each ball once; do not continue hitting until you make each putt.

The putting exercise demonstrates how we are thinking and feeling through a series of different approaches.

CHALLENGE QUESTIONS

- Are your intentions, goals, and targets clear?
- Do you picture your success?
- What might be restricting you from enhancing your target?
- Is there more than one way to achieve your primary goal?

Copyright Performance In Motion 2001

	Score	Thinking	Feeling	Believing	Totals
Regular Way	3 ft Score				
	6 ft Score				
	9 ft Score				
Eyes Closed	3 ft Score				
	6 ft Score				
	9 ft Score				
Looking at Hole	3 ft Score				
	6 ft Score				
	9 ft Score				
One Hand	3 ft Score				
	6 ft Score				
	9 ft Score				
To Club	3 ft Score				
	6 ft Score				
	9 ft Score				

Copyright 2001 Performance In Motion

Before you start, think of some interfering thoughts that you have in business, golf, or other sports that you want to overcome. Start by putting three times from the three-foot distance using your "regular way" of putting. After you have finished those three putts, pick up your score-card and fill in the first line of the chart, going across the page. For Score, write down the number of putts that went in the hole from that distance (0, 1, 2, or 3). The Thinking, Feeling (Physical), and Believing sections in the chart can be filled in with just a few words. We shall see that the creative process involves more than just having a new idea—it is also about turning the idea into action. High performers must trust their ideas and stay with them.

Under Thinking, fill in what your thoughts were while putting. For example, are you thinking about hitting the ball straight? How hard to hit it? That you're not a golfer? What's on the dinner menu? The report you gave last week?

In the Feeling section, note what your body was telling you. Were your arms tense or relaxed? How about your shoulders? Did your grip on the putter feel comfortable or awkward? When you putted, was your putting motion jerky or smooth?

Finally, under Believing, simply note if you believed you could make the shot at the given distance with a simple "yes" or "no."

After doing this quick fill-in of your scorecard, move the balls six feet from the hole and repeat the process, again filling in the chart after you've hit the three balls. If you're finding it difficult to put in words what you're thinking and feeling, just do the best you can. It becomes easier with time.

Finally, move the balls nine feet from the hole, putt the balls, and fill in the chart.

For totals, simply add the total number of putts you sank putting your "regular way." For example, if you made two putts at three feet, one at six feet, and zero putts at nine feet, your total at the far right would be $2 + 1 + 0 = 3$.

Continue the exercise exactly the same way as you hit the ball with four different approaches. First, hit the putts from the three different distances with your eyes closed, pausing to fill out your scorecard. Then, putt the nine strokes while looking at the hole instead of the ball. Third, putt using only one hand (you can choose which hand). Finally, lay a golf club next to the hole and hit to the golf club, aiming for the face of the golf club—the part that strikes the ball—instead of the hole. Fill in the chart for each distance and each technique and tally your scores.

LOOKING AT THE RESULTS

As you look over the results you recorded on the chart, ask yourself the following questions:

What surprised you about this putting exercise?

How did your scores from your "regular way" of putting compare to your other scores?

Was it difficult to stay focused on the target? If so, in what way?

In which way of putting were you most relaxed?

How did your thinking change as you performed the different ways?

How did the physical feel change as you performed the different ways?

How did your believing change as you performed the different ways?

If you did this with others, could you tell if their movement changed?

If you're are like most people, you'll find that your "regular way" of putting—the accepted way, the way you've learned to do things, or the way you believe is the "right way" because of others—is not the only way, nor is it always the most successful way to putt. In fact, after keeping track of scores for over 10,500 participants who have done this putting exercise in my workshops over the last several years, less than 1 percent do better the traditional way they believe it should be done. That means that 99 percent of the people, golfers and non-golfers alike, putted better when they didn't putt in their regular fashion. Or, to put it a little differently, 99 percent of the people had better results when they changed the way they putted.

This demonstrates that people do not become better putters by practice alone but rather by changing their mindsets and recognizing what they are thinking so they can make the change. Once people recognize that change works, they are more open to new ideas and possibilities on and off the course. The mark of a creative golfer, in this case, is not a different way of doing but rather a different way of being. It is about learning to listen both to others and ourselves and to see when we are stuck in old ways of looking at things. It is about understanding the creative process and using it in our lives with a new attitude.

Now look back to the challenge you thought of before you started the putting exercise. Do you notice anything different now? How do you want to change?

This exercise encourages you to try new things even when you have conflicting beliefs about whether putting in a new way might interfere with your performance. As more and more balls find the hole, you will develop an appreciation for the unconscious mind and its role in golf. The body just seems to know where the hole is, even if your mind does not. This methodology uses the creative side of the brain, trying new ways of doing things that you might not have dreamed possible. We often think of creativity as a bright idea or an "aha!," but it is much simpler than that. Creativity comes from just doing it; it is embedded in us all. We just get to allow ourselves to let it out.

Creativity is not just a matter of techniques and skills. Of course, techniques are helpful. But, as many of us know, even when we use techniques for creativity something may still be missing. The process of creativity has an underlying

Are you focused on the Target, when performing?

mystery about it. What takes place is still beyond our control and beyond our awareness. It is as though the creative process has a life of its own that is always beyond our grasp. Techniques may take us to the door of the mystery, but a new level of self-understanding is needed to enter more fully into the creative process. We need to learn how to engage and work with this hidden inner dimension (The Creative Manager, Peter Russell and Roger Evans).

The putting technique is unique because it allows people to change on the inside once they've seen that change works on the outside in a safe, stress-free environment. By bringing opposite values together, you can confront the imbalance and understand each value more thoroughly. This does not mean, of course, that you need to putt with your eyes closed or one-handed from now on. It merely frees you from the mindset of your old way of thinking. The goal of this new mindset is to create the pattern of seeing-allowing-acting-achieving.

If you are using this putting exercise to change your mind set on something outside of golf, what are the new ways in which you can look at the situation? Most conflict results from people believing they have a right way to achieve something, which usually comes from experience. What people fail to see is that others may have better ways to achieve the same goal.

 Chris, the owner of a small business, brought his team through our program because he wanted to alter his employees' point of view. His company had experienced very little growth since they opened twelve years ago. He recognized that something needed to change, but he didn't know what to do. As the CEO, he found it difficult to give up control because of an underlying fear that if he did the work would not get done. This fear trickled down to his staff and hindered their own performance. Chris came into the studio for an assessment and discovered that not only did he need to change his mindset, his staff did as well. In the program, we were doing the putting exercise, and Chris made three out of nine putts when he putted in his normal fashion. I then told him to try putting with his eyes closed and to only focus on getting the ball into the hole. Chris was astonished to find himself making eight out of nine putts with his eyes closed. It was a clear demonstration to him of how doing things in a different fashion could change his beliefs once he saw himself have success. He experienced a breakthrough in his thinking and soon found methods he could use to expand his business in ways that he had never considered before. The rest of the team also experienced different ways to perform. This allowed for the creative process to open the staff to new possibilities they had never considered. The company found significant growth for the first time in twelve years. He began to let go and empower his staff to take on a new mindset. As he gave up control, it became easier to coach them and challenge them to take on new responsibilities. They started to achieve things they never imagined were possible.

A few years ago, I held a business retreat with a team from Wells Fargo. The vice president wanted to address some key initiatives that his team needed to change and believed that they should shake up their way of looking at certain issues. So, instead of doing the coaching in my studio, we took the team to a resort in northern Minnesota for a three-day retreat. As most of them were non-golfers, we didn't tell them we were going to play golf. When they arrived, I was there to greet them and explain some of the activities planned for the next few days, one of which was the putting exercise. We started off by having everyone experience the five different ways of putting. As is almost always the case, no one was able to putt best using their regular method. We talked about the process after the exercise, relating the results back to their key initiatives. Everyone agreed that they needed to make some changes and see different possibilities. After the discussion, I took them back out to the putting green to play a competitive putting game. During this game, every single person went back to putting their perceived right way, despite putting better using other methods in the exercise. As I have said, the ball doesn't lie. The fact that they were making putts with their eyes closed and one-handed indicated that their original putting styles might not have been best for them. After the game, we again processed and talked about the results. They all found it interesting that nobody thought to try one of the experimental ways of putting in the actual game. It isn't always easy to change our perceived "best" way of doing things, especially when we feel something is on the line.

We returned to the conference room and discussed how this illustrated a breakdown in the ability to believe in new ways of doing things.

They realized that if they weren't comfortable changing their methods in a putting competition, then they wouldn't change their methods in the workplace either. This conversation provided the breakthrough the group needed. They were able to look differently at the business initiatives, ultimately saving $300,000 in their work.

For the sake of this book, I use the word "breakthrough" to describe that moment that truly alters a person's perception. Breakthroughs happen when we see things differently and go on to achieve our intended result. For more than 99 percent of the people, the putting experience is a true breakthrough. It shows them that people can perform well while using their natural instincts and changing their point of view. Most golfers do not see themselves as being any good with a golf club in hand. Even avid golfers experience this on a regular basis. The putting exercise allows people to see how well they can perform by opening their minds. Their self-image changes in a significant way. If you believe yourself to be average and awkward in anything that you do, how do you expect to become a top performer?

Achieving breakthrough is one thing, but sustaining it is another. Most of us capitalize on a breakthrough because it tends to go away so fast. Most of us have experienced times when we think that we have reached another level, only to come crashing down a short time later. So how do we sustain the breakthrough? We get to pay attention to this every day. Awareness of what you are thinking and feeling and your openness to the possibilities is a start.

In golf and in business, we get to stay open to creative thinking. Many people are very hesitant to engage in experimental activities because they don't always see the "point" of them. The point of the putting exercise is not to encourage you to putt with your eyes closed. It is to get you to see that there are many different ways to face and conquer a target. You never know when you can shift your point of view through motion. Perfection may never be attainable, but you can be open to the possibilities.

Laura came to my program as part of a team-building seminar I was leading for a large Fortune 500 company. Laura's assessment of her current situation was that she was in a dead-end position. Her only option for advancement was to move her family to another part of the country. As she discussed it with me, she told me that her "only choice is to quit and go to another company." She wasn't really in a situation to quit, though (for many reasons), and so was resigned and bitter at having to accept what seemed unacceptable to her. Her family had found themselves in over their heads with house payments from the recession. Her negative mindset about her family's problems led her into other problems that affected her work.

In this case I assigned her the task of thinking of five different ways to address the situation, similar to our five different ways of putting. At first, she was extremely resistant. The only choices she could see were to quit or to stay and be miserable. In her assessment of the situation, the underlying issues were her boredom with what she was doing and a lack of job openings in her department that would provide the same pay. After some prodding, she was able to list out five other ways of addressing her underlying concerns.

I had her write them out:

1) Get a part-time job to augment my income
2) Ask for overtime or additional assignments
3) Talk to my husband about working more hours (he was working part time)
4) Decrease living expenses
5) Sell our home and buy or rent something cheaper

Laura did not like any of these alternatives, but that was not the point of the exercise. The point of the exercise is that whenever you think you only have two alternatives, there may be much more than meets the eye. There are always at least five, and usually there are dozens. Just knowing that there are several ways to address a situation can bring a sense of clarity.

Laura was a bit more open to making her second list of five alternatives. As she thought about how to address the issue of lack of respect and her boredom, she smiled and her face began to glow.

She realized the possibilities:

1) Talk to my boss about getting different and more challenging assignments that allow for advancement
2) Network
3) Join a business association admired by my peers
4) Write an article for the company newsletter to show leadership skills
5) Volunteer to serve on a committee and learn more about the company

Laura realized that this exercise was very much like the putting exercise. She could use different skills, look at things from new perspectives, and perhaps begin to make some changes. The exercise opened up a new world to her.

The same type of experience happened when I was working with a Division I golfer. Luke was going into his senior year at Winthrop University. His dad realized that he was not playing to his full potential under pressure. His average score was 77.3. He thought he had explored all of his options when working on his game, but he remained frustrated when he could not compete at his highest level. When I got the call from Luke, I insisted that he and his dad go through the program together, even though Luke's dad was not a competitive golfer.

We worked on many things throughout the summer to help Luke achieve peak performance. One of the activities Luke got to try was the putting exercise. When putting his regular way, he made five of nine putts. However, when Luke tried the experimental ways of putting, he found himself making more than five. He putted best to the head of a club (eight of nine), but he also showed improvement when looking at the hole instead of the ball. His dad, on the other hand, made eight of nine putts his regular way, looking at the hole, and even with his eyes closed, maintaining high performance, despite changing his methods.

Luke's goal was to win two tournaments in his senior year. Not only did he win two tournaments individually, but his team also won one of the tournaments. His scoring average for the year was 73.1. He was able to define his strategy, become aware of the target through impact, let go of interference, and develop a firm belief in what was possible. These changes in his thinking were very beneficial to his game, even though he was already performing at a high level before these changes.

Whether it is a high-level golfer or a team within a large business, looking at things differently can help people achieve their goals in a very short amount of time.

Are you open to discovering your possibilities?

POSSIBILITY EXERCISE

Think back to the issue you faced before the putting exercise or another issue in your business or golf game about which you feel stuck. Then, just as Laura did, list at least five different ways in which the situation could be improved. You can use this outline or write it out on a separate piece of paper.

DESCRIPTION OF SITUATION:

My current way of dealing with it (this is similar to your "normal" way of putting):

Five different ways of dealing with this situation:

1)
2)
3)
4)
5)

If, like Laura, you find that you don't like any of these ways, you can do the exercise again and again. Your mind will give you possibilities that may seem outlandish or impossible. If doubt appears, remember your putting exercise and your score after using some of the unusual ways of putting. Just as the ball showed you that you can achieve your desired outcome by focusing on the target, you will also be able to achieve your desired outcome in this instance. The possibilities are endless and allow you to use a lot of creativity.

CREATIVE THINKING

Creative thinking is simply finding new and improved ways to do anything. The biggest rewards in business and golf come from finding new ways to do things better. Strengthening your ability to be a creative thinker will aid in whichever endeavors you choose.

Part of creative thinking involves **believing** that something can be done—and can be done better than you originally thought. Believing that something can be done sets the mind in motion and allows your body to carry out the task.

When I started my business several years ago, I primarily worked with golfers or those who wanted to get into golf. There were times, I will admit, when I would think, "Really? Can this person become a golfer?" However, it didn't take long for me and them to discover this doubt wasn't accurate. I trained a person who only had one arm who soon could shoot in the seventies, as well as many who looked as though they had never played a sport in their life but were able to achieve great results in the game. This happened not only because I believed that they could do it, but because they came to believe in themselves. In the beginning my job was to get them to see and believe that they could do something that they didn't think they could do. When you believe that something can be done, your mind goes to work for you and helps you to find ways to do it. Believing that something can be done paves the way for creative solutions.

You can also discover solutions to business problems when you believe. Think of something that you have wanted to accomplish but have felt as though you could not. Make a list of all the reasons why you can do it. Many of us defeat our inner knowledge that we can do something by focusing on why we can't do it. If we wish to allow creativity to flow more freely in all aspects of our lives, we must abandon our pattern of focusing on failure and begin focusing on the target itself.

 Several years ago I worked with a national sales team that sold medical devices. The sales reps came from around the country for a workshop conducted in the Performance In Motion studio. The team had scheduled a six-hour workshop and had already spent a good thirty minutes trying to figure out why they had lost a major hospital account. They had tried talking to the hospital, but they weren't getting any straight answers. The team was frustrated, and they were trying to solve the situation through assumptions, when in truth no one really knew why they had lost the account.

I asked a few questions to get the workshop back on track, but they kept going back to the same topic. So I asked, "How many more hospitals are there in the area you could call on for new business?" Within the same territory there were at least a dozen additional hospitals one of the reps could call on to make up for the one account that was lost. That particular account was out of their control. They did all the work that they could to maintain the client, but it simply did not work out. It was not doing them any good to waste their time trying to figure out why they lost the client when they could be spending their time thinking of new possibilities. The same can happen with golfers as they try to figure out what is wrong with their swing—they lose sight of the target and become stuck on how to hit the ball.

Instead of the team focusing on something over which they had no control—in this case not knowing why they lost the account—I got them to focus on what they could control. They could simply find a new client. While this may seem like an obvious solution, it shows how hard it was for this group to let go of what was a major loss this was to them. It's just one example of how easy it is to let our emotions, egos, and even our desire to solve problems get in the way of what it is we want to accomplish. We let things we can't control get in the way of the things we can control. Once the sales team was able to focus on their new target (other hospitals in the area), they landed enough additional business to exceed the lost account within several months. Asking why was keeping this company stuck in the past. Asking how guided them into the future.

This team had persistence to work with their client and not let go, which is an essential success quality. They simply needed to blend their persistence with a new quality of reframing and defining new possibilities. When they looked at their visions and goals, they realized that any one company did not really matter. What mattered was having the amount of business that it would take to reach their goals.

Ken, a former CEO of Toro Company and now retired, came into my golf studio in the early 2000s and signed up for a six-week program. His experience with coaching and his history of preventing a company from going bankrupt back in the '80s had already given him many strong management skills, but going through our program helped him reinforce these skills and see his goals through a new approach. After he witnessed a breakthrough by connecting his business with the golf activities used in our studio, Ken began to listen to himself and pick up new insights from his vision board. He was able to enhance his vision and apply his focus to his staff. This allowed new ideas to develop and better communication within his team. Upon completion of our program, Toro's stocks rose to new heights. Toro had always sold their products to their loyal small businesses, but they became aware of finding new ways to maintain relationships with these small businesses while establishing new relationships with bigger-box stores, such as Home Depot.

It was the change in point of view of Ken's golf game that allowed him to open up his mind to new thinking. After a coaching session with four other business leaders, Ken decided to go play a round of golf only using four clubs, rather than his entire set. His scores were lower using these four clubs alone, but he began to think of new possibilities for improving his business. Certainly, executives have thought outside the box before, but the staging of this particular activity for what he wanted to achieve in his company and staff happened at a critical time.

Having a vision, seeing the possibilities, and thinking creatively will make you a better businessperson and a better golfer and will help you enjoy your life more fully.

Chapter Three

Developing a Firm Belief in Yourself and Others

Even though most people really don't believe this, you do have the power to control your thoughts. In golf as in life and in business, your belief system is a critical part of your performance. Do you truly believe in the possibility of change? Or are you stuck thinking that your past performance is a predictor for future performance? By becoming aware of your beliefs, you can also recognize that you have the power to change them.

If all of our frustrations in business, in personal goals, or on the course were magically removed from us today, we would soon find ourselves attracting a similar set of problems about something else. Unless we learn how to redirect our focus from unhappy, restless thoughts and emotions and deal with our mind's focus on dysfunctional chatter about our past and future, the problems will continue to reoccur. The stories, people, and experiences may change, but at the end of the day, week, year, and decade the results will be similar.

I am very grateful to have stumbled onto a different way of looking at the game of golf that can be used to help others. Using golf as a venue for looking and changing our methods of thinking has helped many people recognize the need to change in other areas of their lives. In some cases even non-golfers have used these techniques.

The first step to making changes in any situation is awareness that something needs to change. This awareness may show up as frustration, embarrassment, or even boredom. Feeling these emotions in business or in golf can be used to prompt the changes you wish to make.

USE THE POWER OF YOUR MIND

In sports, as well as at work, subconscious thoughts control our success. As we perform tasks, our brains subtly control minute muscle movements that can mean the difference between success and failure. In our training sessions, we do an exercise that demonstrates how with the power of our minds we can even influence the movement of objects. It's simply a way to get people to see the power of intent. It's also about the ability to visualize our target and how easily interference can distract us from it. Once people learn to focus and experience success in this situation, it's easy to extrapolate the process to real-world situations. This notion was introduced to me in 1997 when I was first starting my business. A coach named Jim Earley gave me new insights to really understand who I am and how to focus on my own targets.

There is nothing magical about this exercise; it simply shows that focused thoughts on a target help our brain coordinate our body's movements to get the desired results. Like a guided missile, as long as we keep our thoughts coordinated to hit the target, our mind and body work together to make the adjustments necessary to stay on course.

Coin moving helps us recognize the power of the mind.

COIN MOVING EXERCISE

In this exercise, you will learn to utilize the power of your mind to move a coin while staying focused on a target. You'll need a washer about the size of a quarter and a piece of string, thread, or fishing line about nine inches long. Tie one end of the string to the washer so that you have a pendulum (you can also improvise by taping a quarter to the end of the string).

Sitting down at a table with the picture of the following golf hole in front of you, hold the loose end of the string with your thumb and index finger. Rest your elbow on the table and move your hand so that the coin, when hanging straight down and perfectly still, is resting over the middle of the image pictured below (at the intersection of the north-south and east-west lines). Keep your arm, hand, and fingers relaxed but stationary throughout the exercise. Take the coin with your free hand, pulling it back a few inches along the north-south line, and let it swing forward. As the coin moves back and forth, you are going to change the direction of the coin to move east-west using only your thoughts. Keep your arm, hand, and fingers relaxed but stationary, and visualize the coin changing directions so that it starts moving back and forth along the east-west axis. With concentration and a little time, the coin should start moving from north-south to a small circular motion to finally an east-west direction.

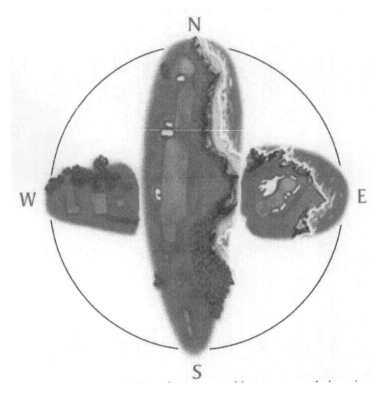

This simple exercise demonstrates the power of intent by showing that your mind alone can make things go in the direction you desire. Once you have the coin moving straight east-west, see if you can change your intent, along with the direction of the coin, by visualizing the coin moving once again along the north-south line. If someone is available nearby, hold the coin back a few inches as before and let it swing from north-south. Have the other person tap the coin with their finger to go east-west. This visually represents interference and distractions that move us in a direction different from our intent. Focus your thoughts again to move the coin north-south. The quicker you can refocus on moving the coin back to north-south, the quicker it will change directions. Focusing on your intent reduces distractions and helps you achieve the results you want.

Now that you have demonstrated to yourself just how much your mind can control, you also get to look at the things that cause you to lose focus. In golf we call these things interference, which can be anything from someone watching you putt, strong winds, or the deliberate interference built into courses, such as bunkers and water. In business, interference can be other people's comments, your memories of past mistakes, or a telephone that keeps ringing. In these and many more instances, you have the opportunity to acknowledge, recognize, and then quickly deal with whatever is causing interference.

DEALING WITH INTERFERENCE

Interference is anything that distracts us from keeping focused on the target. The interference can come from the inside and be self-imposed, as when our own thoughts or actions stray from our goals, or the interference can come from the outside, from someone else's actions or external things, such as weather or road construction. Let's explore some of the ways we encounter interference and how we can deal with it so we can get back on track to staying focused on the target. Interference can be caused by the following (just to name a few):

Focusing on what we don't want to do rather than what we want to do

Allowing the past to control the future

The need for perfection

Negative perceptions clouding our judgment

Chuck, who had recently completed my workshop and had mastered the coin moving exercise, related how he dealt with a frustrating situation while taking a break from the winter cold of Minnesota. Chuck went on a trip to Florida with his family. They decided to spend

one of their days golfing. Because he had learned how to focus and how powerful the mind was, he was able to deal with interference without letting it ruin his game or his day.

I decided to go golfing with my son and wife as a way to relax. Instead of keeping score the regular way, I decided to mark the scorecard with a check if I had a good score on a hole, a dash for an OK hole, and an X for a bad hole. A check mark was not related to the number of strokes I took on any given hole but in my own mind how I played the hole.

The first hole was a disaster, starting with a thirty-yard drive and a ten-yard second shot. I picked up the ball and walked to the green, deciding to practice my putting while waiting for my wife and son to finish the hole. My head was not clearly in the game or focused on a target.

Things got worse at the second tee. This hole—a ninety-degree dogleg that turned sharply at the 150-yard mark— already had two groups ahead of us playing the hole. We waited on the tee box about thirty yards from the first green. A foursome playing behind us approached the green. One of them yelled at us to hit. I responded that we couldn't hit. They kept yelling, and soon we were exchanging some pretty heated words.

It was really up to me to choose how to deal with this distraction. I didn't have to let someone else ruin my day. Taking the time to walk back to the first green where they were putting, I simply pointed out that if they looked ahead more carefully, they would see that we were waiting for two groups ahead of us to move forward before we could hit.

They apologized. Instead of fuming for the rest of the round, I enjoyed the game and did well on the next two holes, rewarding myself with check marks. The next two holes earned dashes, and I finished the round with four more check marks.

By taking control of the situation and not letting myself be victimized, my wife, son, and I could go on and enjoy our game. The exercise simply reminds me of the power I have to choose what to do in the face of interference.

Like some of the best golfers in the world, those in business will face many types of interference on a daily basis. Whether the interference comes from our personal thoughts or from outside influences, as it did in Chuck's story, it takes continued practice and perseverance to stay focused on the outcome you want.

One of my clients noted that his biggest source of interference came from the clients providing the least amount of revenue for his company. After analyzing his customers and his company's use of time, he said, "I've found we've been spending way too much time on the bottom 25 percent of our clients. The clients we work with who bring in the smallest amount of revenue seem to be taking up most of our time. I need to be spending more time with the top 25 percent of our clients to find ways we can help them and in return double our business."

For this business owner it was a particular group of customers that did not fit with the company's profitability goal. By making one decision, by changing one piece of the equation (the bottom 25 percent of the customer base), he removed a major interference to success. The owner discovered how he could keep the company on track, meet his goals, and have more fun doing it. Sure, there are risks involved, and it isn't always easy to let go of what's getting in the way, but the rewards are worth it.

Sometimes the interference can be more difficult to see, especially when it is accompanied by the best of intentions. One of my clients, for example, volunteered her expertise to help on a strategic planning commission for a religious institution. She was totally committed to helping the organization move in the right direction. As she attended the meetings, however, she realized no one had a vision; there was no clear direction for how the group wanted to proceed. Because of this, the well-meaning ideas contributed by others were nothing more than interference. The target wasn't clear, so it was hard for the group to focus. Looking back, she realized she could have saved a lot of time and frustration before she joined by simply asking the group what their vision was. In golf terms, the group needed to decide what the target could be and move forward to play the hole.

What is distracting you at the moment? What is getting in your way of better performance? Is it a disgruntled employee? Is it a product that's taking too much time? Is it lagging sales? Is it pressure from stockholders? Is it an upcoming move or working with vendors who are dragging their feet? Is it something you like to do, or feel like you have to do, that's keeping you from more important matters at hand?

Interference is a daily challenge, and opportunity, whether we create it or something else creates it, is going to confront us even on the way to meeting our smallest goals. The good news is that you have the power to change the direction in which you are moving by changing what you are thinking. While you cannot control the thoughts and actions of others, you can control your own thoughts and actions and how you respond to interference. Changing the direction of something can often be as easy as changing the way you think. Changing your thoughts can change your reality. I often think of the serenity prayer: "God, grant me the serenity to accept the things I cannot change, the courage to change the things I can, and the wisdom to know the difference." This allows us to think and create for ourselves and our teams. It also helps us be open to the mindset to love ourselves in challenging times. You get to be on the planet to grow yourself and others and to make a difference.

One of the ways we experience interference is by remembering events from the past when making decisions in the present. For instance, have you ever thought about why you get mad at yourself after making a mistake or an error in judgment, whether it's on the golf course or in the boardroom? Often we get mad because we're afraid to repeat the same mistake.

When I was playing competitive golf and shooting even par, I went out for a leisurely round of golf with my parents. I played badly on the first two holes, scoring a double-bogey on each hole. I had barely started the game, and already I was four over par. I was fuming mad and decided to stop playing. My thinking was "If I keep shooting like this, there is no way I'm going to score in the thirties for nine holes, or in the seventies for eighteen holes, even if I par every hole from here on out. In fact, I'll be lucky to shoot in the eighties!" So I quit.

As I looked back on this event, I could see how wrong I had been in my thinking. I was angry because I assumed that I would continue to make the same mistakes on the rest of the holes. Why play more holes if they're going to be as bad as the ones I just played? Why repeat the past? What never crossed my mind at that time was that I had also birdied every hole on that golf course at one time or another and so I had the potential to birdie the next sixteen holes. It was a possibility, at least, within the range of my experiences. My record at that point was five birdies in a row. If I had kept playing and birdied the next five holes, simply repeating a positive portion of my past, I would have been one under par after seven holes. Even if I just birdied four of the next sixteen holes and shot par on the rest, I would finish the round even par. Instead, I got mad at myself because I thought I'd make the same mistakes as I had in the past thirty minutes and repeat my poor performance.

Do we really have our eyes open to the possibilities? Or have we let the past control the future?

I tell this story because it is a vivid reminder to me of how powerful our thoughts can be. I could have changed my game, and my performance, by focusing on times when I performed well. Instead, I let the first two holes control my day, and at that moment I made a decision about my future—or the next sixteen holes, at least. I had a choice to let them be an opportunity for success or a chance to fail. I decided I was going to fail and walked away from what could have been my biggest comeback ever.

Letting go of the past is one of the most effective tools in our game and in our life. It allows us to move forward and live in the moment to create our dreams. How quickly are you able to change your thoughts? How fast can you let go of the past and realize you can perform better in the next business meeting, the next phone call, or the next customer interaction? Even if your day started out poorly, that is already in the past. You have the power to create the future. You do not need to become the victim of your own game, thinking that you're trapped in a downward spiral because things started out on a low note. Even though it may be difficult to see at the time, the next moment could be the start of your biggest comeback ever. You have the power to change your future by changing your thoughts.

THE NEED FOR PERFECTION

Perfectionism is always about fear and a lack of confidence. But what is perfection exactly? Does it ever fully exist or last forever? This certainly doesn't mean we can't work toward it every day, but we shouldn't be disappointed if we are not perfect. When we feel that we must do something perfectly, we tend to lack confidence. Where does confidence come from? How do we get it? It certainly does not come from never making a mistake. It comes from learning from our mistakes.

After years of studying many top performers in business, golf, and other fields, they have proven that confidence comes only from within. Friends and family mean well when they say, "It's only in your imagination. There's nothing to be afraid of." You and I know, though, that type of reassurance never works. Such remarks may give us relief for a few minutes, but the truth of the matter is that hearing "It's only in your imagination" doesn't really build confidence or cure fear. Fear is very real and can cripple us. The first step is to recognize it exists, determine where it is coming from, and learn how to deal with it.

We can call this emotion fear, worry, tension, embarrassment, perfectionism, or self-consciousness, but whatever we call it, it can immobilize us. Simply knowing about fear and how we generate it doesn't cure it. Fear is the number one factor in ruining opportunities for success. It wears us down physically and can actually make us sick. It prevents people from achieving what they want. It certainly messes up a wonderful round of golf. Many people know how quickly we can "lose it" when we are playing one of our best rounds ever. We get nervous because we lose our belief and have a need for perfection to finish strong that takes us out of our flow state, or zone.

In golf the first tee often sets up the player for a round of fear. As many people discover in my workshops, when they first do an exercise like putting, there is added pressure and tension when other people are watching. It is the fear of performing well or looking good with someone else watching. Ask golfers where they feel the most pressure to hit a good shot, and most will say on the first tee, because that is where other people are waiting and watching. Focusing on these other people can also cause us to lose the focus on the target itself.

Speaking to groups or giving presentations is one of the greatest fears people have for the same reason—they are afraid of looking bad or making a mistake in front of others. Performing before an audience, whether it's hitting the golf ball or giving a speech to several hundred people, can cause a great deal of anxiety and interference that takes your mind off the target.

The awareness that you are fearful and calling fear by its true name is the first step to making change. The next steps are preparation and understanding that all confidence is acquired and developed through action. No one is born with confidence. Those people you know who radiate confidence, who are on the journey to mastery, are those who acquired their confidence through action.

Positive action helps relieve fear. The motion exercises and activities in this book are one way to build confidence. That is why, in my training, I have people write positive things that happen to them in their workbooks. I then ask them to relate those things to what they are learning.

Action is the cure for fear. I have seen this many times. I had a business owner and her team, who were struggling with sales, into my studio. The fear of the economy and their calls versus sale completion was getting to them. They listed all of their worries to me in great detail. Finally I cut in and asked them, "What are you doing about it? What are you doing to correct this situation? Where would you like to be in a week? A month? Three months? Six months? A year?"

They seemed to think that talking about and worrying about the issue was doing something about it. I decided to demonstrate something to them through the medium of golf.

Most of the people on the team enjoyed golf, so I played a putting competition with them in the studio. However, several weeks before this session, they had participated in the five ways of putting exercise, and many had done better putting with their eyes closed than with them opened. When we competed that day, though, they went back to their regular way of putting. I knew this would demonstrate to them that they had gone back to old thought processes.

After the game I simply asked questions of the group that allowed them to process and make changes in their way of thinking. I was pleased to see confidence return to their eyes. They were soon taking action steps. They realized that they had been over controlling other members and were micromanaging. They laid out a plan for leadership and sales teams. Soon thereafter, the business owner and her staff began to achieve their goals as they were able to become creative leaders as a team.

Much lack of self-confidence can be traced back to a mismanaged memory. Memories are just things we deposit in our brains. Often we don't deposit what is really true. We, of course, don't always have control over our experiences, but we do have control over how we remember them and the stories we tell ourselves about our experiences. Are your stories about golf and other areas of your life confident or self-demeaning? Your brain will remember what you tell it to remember. Confident, successful people specialize in putting positive thoughts into their memory banks. You are always telling yourself the story of your life. Make sure to tell it in positive terms.

There are many ways in which you can put positive thoughts in your mind. Driving a car, eating alone, or taking a shower are all good opportunities to feed your mind positive thoughts. Before you go to bed at night might be the best time to plant your positive thoughts and images in your mind. Review your accomplishments and victories during the day and ask yourself what you are grateful for and how you would like to get more out of them. Take a week to replay the memories you create for yourself. Then, take another week and replace the negative memories with positive ones. See how much better you feel and perform in just a few weeks of changing your self-talk.

PERCEPTIONS RESTRICTING THE REALITY

What do you see as you approach your shot?

Is your perception true to reality? How do past experiences influence how you think today? Do you perceive a golf hole with a water hazard as harder to play than one without water? Or do you play the same shot to the same hole over and over again? Pretend that you are going to play the hole below in your mind. What do you see?

It is not unusual to get into a situation where perception is different from reality. You expect one thing, and something entirely different occurs. You procrastinate on a big project, for example, because the perception is that it not going to be overwhelming, unmanageable, and a grind to get through. When you finally start, however, you discover it was easier than you thought. Whether it is lack of awareness, a shortage of information, or a misconception on one's part, the perception we have of a situation does not always give us an accurate picture of reality.

Without looking at the picture again, answer the following questions:

1. What is the color of the flag?
2. What is the color of the flagstick?
3. Where is the flagstick (pin) located in relation to the rest of the green? Front? Center? Back? Left? Right?
4. How many sand traps are there?
5. Where exactly did you want to hit your shot?
6. The picture below is the same golf hole you saw earlier, this time looking back at the house from behind the green.

Our perceptions may be different than the reality

Now take a minute to look back at the picture of the golf hole from the tee box. Pretend you've just hit your shot.

The picture on the right is the same hole. Many people are not aware of the sand trap on the right of this flag stick from the tee box (picture on the right); looking down (picture on the left) you don't see the sand trap.

Looking at the hole from this perspective, how do you see the hole now?

These pictures raise many important lessons about perception and awareness. First, what we see initially is not always true to reality. People think of a golf course when they see the hole from the tee box. They only see what they see, which is not always the reality. We also usually do not see the target we want to hit, even when we think we do.

Where else do you recognize that perception is different than reality in business, your personal goals, and golf?

This exercise helps people become more aware of their surroundings. It is the awareness that is the first step to improving performance.

Let's say a marketing director of a company is working with a long-term mindset, setting out goals that can be achieved within two years. At the same time, the sales director may be operating with a shorter-term mindset that covers a three-month span. Two separate mindsets from two company leaders will complicate the situation and confuse other employees, which will hurt the company in the future.

The snow gives an opportunity to use the environment to one's advantage.

When looking at it from a different angle, reality becomes clear.

Here is another example of perception versus reality. The two pictures above were taken in Minnesota in April. I challenged a number of people to get the ball onto the green. Being a fairly small green with snow surrounding it, the perception of each person was that they needed to be precise with the tee shot. However, the reality was that they could hit a putt and bank the ball off of the snow, all the way down to the green, and do it fairly easily. Taking in the whole environment before stepping up to the ball would have made a big difference. Have we really explored all the possibilities before we seek to perform?

OVERCOMING A SELF-DEFEATING PERCEPTION

 Our perception in one area of our life can affect our performance in other areas. Julie, for example, was a non-golfer and manager with a large insurance company. She was a quick learner and very smart. During a putting exercise in the studio, she suddenly stopped putting and said out loud, "I can't putt. I am not an athlete." She was frustrated, and I sensed some anger riding underneath her comments as she set her putter to the side. An invisible wall went up in front of her, and the relaxed environment of the group suddenly changed, as though a black cloud had hit the inside of the studio.

I wasn't exactly sure what Julie was thinking, but I knew she was not open to the possibilities. A perception was getting in her way. Getting her to change her thought process would be an opportunity for a breakthrough.

I handed Julie a few golf balls, backed up three feet, put my hand up as a target, and said, "Julie, toss me a golf ball." She threw it to me with her left hand, even though she was right-handed. She hit the target. I backed up three more feet. "Toss me another one." She threw another one underhand, this one with her right hand and directly on target. I took a long stride backward and raised my hand, nine feet away. Again, without hesitation, she hit the target.

"When you threw me the golf ball just now, what did you do physically," I asked, "with your arm?"

"I moved my arm forward toward the target," she replied.

"Right. Now grab a putter and make the same forward motion with your hands, without hitting a ball. In other words, simply pretend you're tossing me the ball while swinging the putter, remaining focused on the target."

Julie took a few practice swings with the putter.

I set the head of the golf club I was holding down on the ground, three feet in front of her, and said, Now move the putter the same way you just did, aiming for my club with a golf ball."

Julie putted the ball and it hit my club.

"Interesting," I said, backing up another five feet and setting my club in front of a hole. "Hit the club again." Julie took aim and hit the club squarely with her putt. "Now put the ball in the hole," I said as I took away my club. She aimed, hit the ball, and drained the putt. She was now smiling and engaged, having discovered she could putt after all.

What had happened? Two things were going on in Julie's head that stopped her from participating. First, she was most likely getting negative signals from past experiences in sports. "I can't compete as an athlete. I am not coordinated. I'm not going to do something if I can't succeed, whether it's golfing or badminton." Second, interfering thoughts were getting in the way. "If I can't put the ball in the hole, I must be doing something wrong. If I can't do something right it means I'm a failure." As in many cases, this was a great correlation to the issues she faced in the office. I thought, "What are the questions she can ask herself when she is in a similar situation in order to overcome it?"

As a coach, I helped Julie see that putting was as easy as tossing a ball, which she already knew how to do. This changed her perception from "This is something I can't do" to "This is something I can do." I also guessed that the hole was creating interference (putting and success equals getting the ball in the hole), so I took the hole out of the equation by having her aim for my golf club instead. The purpose was to show her that she could succeed in hitting a target without having the ball go in the hole. After a few successes, knowing she could hit a target, the hole no longer became an obstacle for Julie. It wasn't about good or bad, right or wrong; it was simply about putting the ball to a hole. The breakthrough for her was realizing that she could be very focused and achieve things she did not think were possible, while remaining unattached to the things she could not control.

FEAR OF FAILURE AT WORK

This well-choreographed dance occurs daily in the workplace. Employees or managers start out with a perception and suddenly equate that perception with "I can't do my job." Because they don't want to be the one making all the mistakes, or they are fearful they may look stupid or lose their job, they stop taking chances, or blame others, or shut down. Soon an invisible wall pops up, all because of the wrong perception. This is not just with employees or middle managers; this can happen with leadership teams, executive teams, CFOs, and CEOs. The role of a good coach is to help them see this is happening without telling them what to do.

Creating awareness or a new perception is often the first step in overcoming such obstacles. Going back to the example of Julie, when we discussed what happened with putting and related it to her work, she agreed that when she encounters a new situation that seems overwhelming, her first thought is often "I can't do this." Putting gave her a new perspective that allowed her to look at other possibilities without closing down so quickly. Now, when faced with a new situation, thinking back to other projects or situations where she has succeeded and done well in the past, like knowing she can toss a golf ball, may be all it takes to change her perception into "I know I can do this because I've done something like it before." Julie might think of this by herself, or she may need a reminder from her manager about similar situations where she has succeeded.

In any business situation, you may have as many different perceptions as you have people involved. Even though a foursome of golfers or a team of employees is looking at the same hole or project, what we each see is influenced from experiences we've had in the past. So our viewpoints may be very different. We can't assume everybody sees the same thing or is on the same page. It is helpful, therefore, to see if your perceptions match those of others and be aware of what's happening "around the hole" that could affect the outcome.

CHANGING OUR PERCEPTIONS

Many years ago I had a high school student come to me to improve his golf game. Although he was good enough to be on the junior varsity golf team, he admitted he was "probably the worst golfer on the team" and was ready to quit. His best score for eighteen holes was a ninety-seven, and he rarely broke fifty for nine holes.

It did not take long for me to see that Jason's golf scores were directly connected to the perceptions he had about competitive golf and his fear of failure. While his coaches wanted to help him with the fundamentals, Jason got nervous when his coaches were watching, tensing up on the swing and hitting the ball poorly. His coaches tried to fix his swing—what they saw from the outside—instead of taking time to realize Jason's swing was simply the result of his negative thinking. The doubt was created by lack of focus and loss of his target through impact.

It was important for Jason to deal with failure as an opportunity to learn from what happened, to change the things he could change, to refocus, and to let go of the past. "Dan didn't even teach me the fundamentals," Jason recalls, "but my swing improved through awareness and focus on the target. He taught me how to feel the club in my hands and how to create different kinds of shots." Two weeks later, after just two sessions, Jason shot his career round for nine holes of thirty-seven, just one over par.

Instead of dreading the upcoming golf season as a sophomore, Jason was excited. "I have a whole new outlook on golf," he said. "I am no longer afraid of failure, and my swing feels confident. I lowered my score, on average, by nineteen strokes." Jason's golf continued to improve as a junior and senior, scoring low rounds of seventy-two for eighteen holes and thirty-three for nine holes. This became an opportunity for him to be mindful of what he was experiencing on the course, which later changed the course of his life.

However, the most noticeable benefits of Jason changing his perception happened off the golf course. When we first met, Jason couldn't look me straight in the eyes because of his low self-esteem. Now at school he began taking on leadership roles in extracurricular activities and gained more confidence as a speaker. His grades also improved. His average grades of Bs when we first started working together changed to As in high school, where they remained throughout college, even with a double major.

"I sat down with Dan to look at my goals for my first semester in college," Jason remembered as a smile settled on his face. "He asked me what grades I wanted to get. I knew I became a pretty good student in high school but didn't know what to expect in college, so I marked down three As and an A- for my goals. The A- was to give myself permission to not have to be perfect. Not only did I get three As and an A-, my A- was just one point away from getting another A. I don't consider myself superstitious, but Dan keeps saying that if you write down what you want, you often get it. The following semesters I didn't make the same mistake—I wrote down all As and achieved it. More important than the grades, however, is the confidence I've gained through what

I've learned with Dan. I look forward to applying the same concepts to my career and future life."

By changing his perception, Jason not only changed how he looked at things but broadened his opportunities and changed his life into something better than he had ever imagined. At the time of this writing, Jason is attending Harvard to work on his doctorate degree.

Asking questions of others to understand their perceptions can be helpful in terms of customers, clients, or competition. Do your customers perceive the benefits of your product or service the same way you do? What are the perceptions of your core audience to your company and product? Do you assume all your customers have the exact same needs? Do you proactively ask your customers what their needs are?

There is perhaps no other sport in which your mental game is more important than golf. Mastering your thoughts will aid in your golf game, and learning how to do so will improve your work and your life.

3 pictures from different angles show multiple perceptions of the same golf hole.

MANAGING YOUR MINDSET

If our mindsets have such a powerful effect on us, then wouldn't it just be better to get rid of them in order to eliminate the ups and downs of performance? It might seem like it, but the answer is no. Mindsets bring order to our lives and help us decide what to do in certain situations. The mindset helps us interpret the picture or movie of the world. Without it, we would see nothing.

It is important to understand that mindsets are not good or bad, right or wrong. The real issue is whether we are clear with them. If we understand them, then we can make the necessary changes. When our perceptions are different from our realities, that is when we find ourselves in trouble. Sometimes, mindsets can limit our boundaries and only allow us to see part of the bigger picture.

To what extent does your mindset help you become the master? To what extent does it put you as the victim? To be in control of our own mindsets helps us see, think, influence, behave, and perform.

Chapter Four

Developing Focus

There will be many things that distract us from our desired intentions. In golf and in business, the interference must be identified in order to allow ourselves to focus on our critical targets. Those of you who have tried to play golf when you have other things on your mind know what I am talking about. There are so many things that can happen to us during the day. The ability to focus on what is important—the target and the goal—is the key to clear these mental ruminations before we play. The mind must be free for the body to perform in peak performance. It also must be clear on where you are headed and what you want to achieve.

Jack Nicklaus was always trying to understand who he was as a person to achieve his great results on the course. Back then, they didn't know how to explain the value of the mind and body working together, so most of the information people interpreted was from his golf swing. Today, we realize we can learn more from what people are thinking than from what they are doing. Their thoughts have an effect on their actions, and recognizing these thoughts is the key to understanding their behavior.

Years ago I was out on the course for a nine-hole coaching session with Wes. He wasn't playing very well, so I asked him if he had anything on his mind. He said yes and that his mother was not feeling very well. Clearly, Wes's concern for his mother was pulling on him, and his attention was so directed toward her that he was not focusing on the round. His game was a mess after three holes, and I suggested that he contact his mom on the course. A quick telephone call told him that she did, indeed, need his help later in the afternoon but didn't know how to get a hold of him. As soon as Wes was able to clear up the interference of thinking about his mother, he could concentrate on the game at hand. He still had time to play the six remaining holes before his mother needed him. What was fascinating was to see how Wes played the back nine compared to his initial distracted play of the front nine. By connecting to the main source of his distraction and taking a simple step to be more aware of what he could control and what he couldn't, Wes became clear about his game and improved his score. He also told me that he was later able to interact with his mother with more compassion and clarity. The pattern interrupt on the course allowed Wes to be more present.

Just as an individual's success on the golf course is directly proportionate to his or her ability to solve any issues that arise, the same holds true for any company or business. The opportunity is the awareness of making the change so you can take your game to new heights on and off the course. In time, you can become great at identifying these opportunities, discussing them honestly, and addressing them immediately. By dealing with the distractions and key issues we become very focused on our goals.

CLUB THROWING EXERCISE

One way I coach golf students to focus is by having them throw old clubs. In order to do this, the clubs are wrapped with a padded material (so that you don't harm yourself or others as you throw). If you want to do this, just make sure your clubs are padded or that where you are throwing the club is wide open. I learned the club throw technique from Fred Shoemaker of Extraordinary Golf. The club throw technique allows you to see that by truly focusing on your target you can hit it. While focusing on your target, your swing can and will change naturally. People tend to think about what went wrong with their swing—or the process—and ignore the fact that they did not have a clear idea of where they wanted the ball go to.

Again, most people in golf look to what is wrong with their swing before understanding what they might be thinking. The mind is always involved. To get enjoyment out of golf, for instance, one certainly does need skills. This set of skills requires the ability to focus on a target and let go of interference. It is important to think about your desire to learn about the various aspects of the game—thoughts, skills, feelings, and why you are even playing in the first place. It is impossible to achieve the discipline necessary to learn to golf well enough to fully enjoy it. You will score lower but not necessarily enjoy the game more. The enjoyment takes place in the mind for the golfer. The flow with the motion cannot be purely physical; there has to be a connection with the mind.

 Mark, a local news reporter in Minneapolis at the time, was doing a story on my business a few years ago. After going through a few of the exercises and interviewing some of my clients, he saw that my program could improve his golf game—primarily his swing. After seeing the story, Mark's wife knew that he needed to make a change with his current job situation and encouraged him to go through my program focusing on his work as well.

Mark had loved his job at the station and was very good at telling the story within the news. He worked there for eighteen years but was seeking new ways to add to his income so his wife would not have to travel as often for her job and could spend more time with their kids. As with all of our clients, we highly customized the Discovery Series for Mark, working on several techniques to help him focus on his goals and vision. Not long after, I had him try the club throw technique. The aim of the activity was to help him focus on the target in golf and become more aware of his swing as he focused on the target.

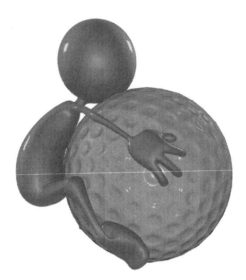

Too many people get stuck
At the ball vs. focused on the
Target while performing.

Club-throwing brings out the natural swing when the individual is focused on the target

The club throw allowed him to focus on the target and let go of being stuck at the ball. This would also help him relate to other goals in his life. First, we captured his swing on camera as he swung and hit the golf ball. Next, I gave him an oversized club and asked him to focus on a target. I then told him to throw the club at his target so we could capture his natural balance on film. Mark's natural swing emerges as he throws the clubs toward his target. The pictures below tell the story.

Captions for the photos above, starting top left, going to the right, and then downward. The ball hitting photos are labeled with letter A. Club throw photos are labeled with B.

<u>Setup</u>
A: Tense and tight; head down
B: Relaxed and balanced; focused on target

<u>Backswing</u>
A: Weight on left knee; out of balance
B: Weight balanced over back leg

<u>Top of backswing</u>
A: Stuck at the ball; end outside of right foot and into left knee
B: Upper and lower body working together; weight over right foot and balanced

<u>Halfway down</u>
A: Weight moving upward
B: Weight transferring forward; upper and lower body moving together

<u>At impact</u>
A: Not engaged with target
B: Relaxed and engaged with target; increased power

<u>Finish</u>
A: Tense; body doesn't fully release to the target
B: Relaxed and releasing to the target

What I have realized over all of these years is that the golf swing is like a person's fingerprint. There are as many ways to swing the club as there are people. Yes, there are certain fundamentals that apply to every high-performing golfer, like a good useful finger or hand would look like. But when we break things down, there are many different styles to get the job done.

Once Mark realized the importance of focusing on the target in golf, he began to see how he could apply the same principles to his work and personal life. He began to rethink what was really important to him and his family and how he could change things up. He had already hit the maximum income level for his skill level at his position and realized it would be difficult to make any more money. It was time for him to move on to a job outside the company. That became his target—something he was able to achieve—and gave his wife the ability to be home with their growing family.

As I worked with this technique over a few years, I realized that it could be applied to many situations in which you are seeking to improve your focus. Research proves that intelligence does not necessarily lead to smart thinking. To think effectively is the result of seeing your target while in the performance state, such as focusing on where you want to drive your car down the road.

In many businesses, for example, when they recognize the need to improve their use of time, they focus in on time management programs. They feel the change needs to come from the outside instead of within, which is where the club throw technique comes into play. It is a great demonstration of how changing the mind by connecting to the target can lead to rapid and dramatic results.

Studies also show that the brain or mind is like a muscle. The more you use it, the stronger it will become. Training it to see things that other people don't see develops a natural reflex that allows you to do this on a regular basis. In my studio, I have a picture of a golf hole on the wall. I tell people to imagine that they are playing the hole, but they can seldom recall the color of the flag or stick after they have made the shots in their minds.

It is also important to understand that the unconscious mental processes are hidden from our awareness. It is the mind and the body that connects the club throw to the target. Similar to the mental images comprising your vision board, they all fit together to define the target. Seeing images of success on your vision board will help you get there, just like seeing the target while throwing clubs will direct the club to where you want it to go.

Sometimes we can too easily override the target and instead rely on grip, stance, and swing. As I have mentioned, being a member of the PGA, I was trained to work with the conscious mind on these types of mechanics. The techniques I was taught to teach others were very good when it came to rational thinking, analysis, and planning of the golf swing, but what was ignored was how to get people to understand the unconscious process. Hoping that the mind and body come together after learning about swing mechanics is not an effective way to improve.

Exercises like club throwing remind us of the power of a precise target. Instead of staying stuck in the how, we trust more in the innate tools we already have. By focusing on the target and relaxing, we can gain confidence and increase performance in everything we do. At times, I will take small groups out to local golf courses, country clubs, etc., and have them practice on focusing on the target, understanding interference, and then removing the interference to meet specific goals. With one such group I added the extra challenge of limiting the number of golf clubs each person could use. I let some use several clubs, but one person—a college golfer—I only let use a seven-iron on every shot. The initial goal was to hit the golf ball and get it as close to the pin on the green as possible. While all the holes were par-three, several were close to two hundred yards in length, making it a challenge for everyone in the group. Luke, the college golfer, was able to score one under par while playing a game he never imagined.

Rick, who was a manager with a large accounting firm, started out poorly during one of our on-course playing sessions and went downhill from there. Though he was a golfer, he kept losing the target and hitting the ball off course. After several holes, Rick was extremely frustrated as his shots kept getting worse, even though he had just purchased an expensive set of new golf clubs. Adding insult to injury was the college student who was shooting under par, despite the fact that he was only using the one club (even when putting on the green). It was clear that Rick had lost his focus.

When I could see that Rick was completely distracted and checked out of his game, I had him try a different strategy in the middle of his round. Since it appeared that all the interference for Rick happened when he was hitting the golf ball, I simply removed the ball from the equation. I asked him instead to pick one of the new clubs out of his bag, aim it at the pin on the green, and throw it. The first club he threw fell and landed fifty yards behind him and was stuck in a tree (this became a story within the story—but that is for another time). I reminded him to focus on the target, which was the flag, keeping his eye on the color of the flag even when following through with his club throw. The next four clubs went straight in line with the pin (still ending up short, intending not to ruin the green).

I put a golf ball on the tee, and I asked Rick a few questions to help him stay focused: What was the color of the flag? The flagstick? Where did he want the ball to land on the green? When he answered, he sounded confident. He kept focused on the target, just as he had when throwing the last few clubs, and kept the target in his mind as he hit the ball. He hit the ball, and it landed on the green four feet from the hole, his best shot of the day. What was more important, however, was that he understood how this change happened, and others saw it too.

Throwing the golf club for Rick helped him learn to relax in a performance situation, which for him was hitting the ball when others were watching. With further coaching, Rick, who usually shot in the one hundreds for an eighteen-hole round, was soon hitting in the eighties.

More importantly, he started transferring the skills of relaxing and focusing on the target under pressure from the golf course to his job. He became more focused on what he was doing at work, asking key questions of his coworkers in order to pull out answers. This increased his confidence. As he earned respect from others and demonstrated his coaching skills, he received a promotion within six months.

In coaching Rick on his golf game, I found that removing the ball enabled him to focus on his swing and removed the interference, which for him was hitting the ball while others watched. Once he could relax and trust his natural swing, he began to use the gifts he had lost under the pressure of improving what he felt was his lousy performance. In any situation, we can be distracted and forget to draw upon our natural abilities.

People enjoy throwing clubs. It is different, and since there's no right or wrong way to do it, they can focus on the target without judgment. This helps them relax, open up, and literally let go, which gives a more natural swing with more power. As good coaches know, athletes perform at the top of their game when they are relaxed. Michael Phelps comes to mind with his ever-present iPod at the 2008 Olympic Games in Beijing, listening to music as he calmed himself before his swimming events and taking home eight gold medals. Whether you're swimming, golfing, or working, you perform better when your muscles are relaxed. It is a matter of thinking less and trusting more as you allow your subconscious to be applied to the target.

This is just one of the exercises that can be used in a variety of ways to help people recognize and remove interference in their own lives. This process allows people to find their target, focus, and build on the strengths that come naturally to them.

The same is true in business. You perform better when you are relaxed. It helps you play into your strengths in very challenging environments. In the early years of my program, I had a few sessions working with an anchorwoman from a Minneapolis news station to help improve her golf game. The real benefit of the program for her, however, was that the ball hitting and club throwing exercises at the studio helped decrease her anxiety while doing the evening news on television.

Instead of focusing on how nervous she was or how many people were watching her or instead of trying to duplicate techniques used by her peers, she learned to relax and focus on the target and the things she could control—telling the best news story possible in her own, authentic style. Playing her own game—using her own skills and talent—made her less nervous, more relaxed, and therefore more engaged with her audience.

In business, keeping your thoughts on what you want to say—on your message—and then listening to the needs of others will help you relax, listen to others, and remove interference. Whether the interference comes during a job interview, asking a question at a team meeting, or giving a keynote presentation, you will always perform better when you are focusing on a target and not when you are focusing on what others are thinking about you.

When people are under pressure or performing below their potential, they usually don't realize what's happening. In other words, just like Rick, they know they aren't performing as they should, but they can't explain why. The explanation, though, is that they have somehow turned their focus away from their target and toward something else. Changes in awareness often happens at a subconscious level. Sometimes it takes a coach to point out the source of the interference and teach people how to identify it for themselves. When people can begin to pay attention to what is natural and what is unnatural for them in terms of their thoughts and feelings, they can make huge breakthroughs.

In the studio, we teach target, focus, relaxing, and releasing when throwing the club. Once you pick a specific target, for example the red flag on the yellow pin on the green, you keep this image focused in your mind as you relax and swing then release the club and let it go.

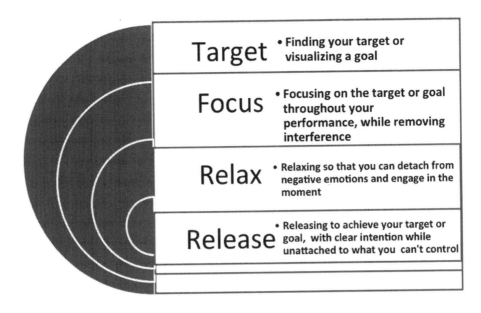

Target • Finding your target or visualizing a goal

Focus • Focusing on the target or goal throughout your performance, while removing interference

Relax • Relaxing so that you can detach from negative emotions and engage in the moment

Release • Releasing to achieve your target or goal, with clear intention while unattached to what you can't control

For Rick, the importance of the club throwing exercise was not just the follow-through but also reconnecting himself to the target. In other words, Rick needed to keep his eyes on the target from start to finish until he saw the club hit the target. On the golf course, if he could keep the image of the target in his mind through impact, the ball went on target. If he lost the image of the target in his mind before he actually finished following through the shot with the golf club, the ball did not go where he wanted. Just practicing this one thing helped Rick eventually lower his scores by having a clear target and dealing with interference. In business, he needed to remember that it was not enough simply to focus on a target; he had to keep the target constantly in mind until he accomplished his goal.

YOU HIT WHAT YOU FOCUS UPON

 Loren had two passions: motorcycling and golf. While he loved to golf, his score always hovered around the one hundred mark. He came to my program after his wife gave it to him as a present, uncertain if anything could really improve his game. After completing it, though, he told me that learning to focus had made an amazing difference in how he viewed playing golf. "Why," he wondered, "had I never considered that focusing on a target was the way to play golf?" He continued, "When I first started to ride a motorcycle, I took a motorcycle safely course. One of the things they taught us was that we should never focus on the debris in the road. We were told that, no matter what the obstacle (roadkill, stones, and branches on the road), we would drive directly into it if we focused on it. Instead, we were taught to focus on the path that we wanted our bike to take around the obstacle. It makes perfect sense that if I focus on the obstacles in my path in golf (such as water hazards, bunkers, etc.) I will drive my ball directly into them."

One can remain focused on the target when they override interference.

The obstacles and interference in our golf games and our business lives get a lot of attention. It often seems as if it is impossible to ignore these things. In golf many of these hazards have been intentionally placed there to distract us from our focus. But in reality as a kid many of us played on the beach and in the water. In business, these things seem almost intentional sometimes. But, if we learn to focus on our target and not on the interference, we are highly likely to achieve our desired outcomes.

Chapter Five

Partnership of Mind and Body—The Flow State

Focusing on a specific target, relaxing, and following through helps the mind and body to naturally compensate to help you hit a target in golf. The same principle applies to almost anything you do in life. However, a word of caution: what I've discovered from my own experience and coaching throughout the years, whether with golfers, managers, or CEOs, is that it is easy for all of us to lose the focus of the target very quickly. Often, our minds can go into the subconscious to allow our bodies to remember how to do things, even when our environment is clouded. The ability to remain flexible and open to change is the key to many top performers.

The need for inner flexibility does not conflict with the need for inner stability; each depends upon the other. If we cannot maintain an inner calm, we may find ourselves clinging to set patterns of behavior for a sense of security. On the other hand, if we are at peace within, we are much freer to respond to change and to respond more appropriately.

Being flexible means simply adapting to changing conditions while remaining focused on the goal/end in mind.

In this chapter we will discuss the wisdom of the body and how our bodies will respond even when our minds may not be cooperating.

OPENNESS TO CHANGE

Most of us have difficulty believing in what we cannot see. Kelly, for example, knew she wasn't where she wanted to be with her golf game. She loved the game of golf and was shooting in the mid to upper eighties by the time she was a freshman in high school. Her teacher was working hard on the mechanics of Kelly's golf swing, but it didn't seem to be helping. Kelly had made a few swing changes that helped her improve, but she got to a point where she was stuck and could no longer improve by changing technique alone. Her scores on the course were not improving; in fact, they were getting worse. More importantly, Kelly wasn't enjoying the game as she had in the past and was frustrated. She knew she had to make some changes.

Kelly's brother read an article about my business and gave me a call. After talking, he suggested to Kelly that she meet with me.

During our first session, I could see that Kelly was worrying about the mechanics of her swing. She was tense and anxious, her head full of negative thoughts when she was striking the ball. After a few motion exercises in the studio, Kelly began to relax and have fun. By focusing on the target rather than the mechanics of how she thought she should be swinging the club, Kelly quickly discovered new ways in which she could hit the ball without being told how to do it. She learned how to become her own coach in a way that felt natural and intuitive rather than forced. She left the studio that day with a smile on her face.

Two weeks later Kelly played in a golf tournament and won, hitting all eighteen greens in regulation and scoring a one-under par seventy-one. After the tournament she called me to talk about her experience. She said, "I never realized I could have so much fun playing golf." It was also the first time Kelly felt comfortable having her mom watch her play in a golf tournament.

Getting Kelly to believe in herself and in her new authentic swing was not an instant change. It took the rest of the summer coaching Kelly to become aware of what was restricting her before she could implement long-term changes in her golf game. But after looking at where she was and where she wanted to be, Kelly had the courage to change her swing and continue her training with me. These changes ultimately helped Kelly reach her larger goal of going to college and playing golf at Montana State. She went on to become the number one player on the team, but the skills she had learned weren't just about golf. She also became skilled at managing what was important in her life and what was not.

Sometimes we need to start over from a new perspective because we are too close to our own problems. Throughout the years, we have used my golf studio as a retreat center for many to back away from their situations and begin to see new possibilities.

Dealing with change and flexibility are not only two key ingredients in the management of change, but they are also intrinsic to creativity. The creative person is not panicked by new situations and challenges but can step back and see them with fresh, artistic eyes. To manage the future successfully requires innovative thinking and a willingness to look at new responses. The challenges of the twenty-first century will require us to draw upon our creative resources like never before. One of the creative resources at our disposal is to tap into the wisdom of our physical bodies. Our bodies are often aware of issues, problems, and strengths that our conscious minds have not incorporated.

BEHAVIORAL KINESIOLOGY EXERCISE

Kinesiology is the study of the mechanics of body movement and the application of that study to the treatment of imbalance throughout the body. It is basically a verification tool that helps us find where we are "off track" and where we need to pay attention. Kinesiology is a gentle, noninvasive method of identifying what is going on and why and then applying suitable techniques to restore a sense of well-being. Through the use of kinesiology, we can demonstrate the powerful effect that words and energy have on our body.

Kinesiology, sometimes called "muscle testing," involves testing the body's responses when applying slight pressure to a large muscle. It is often used to provide information on energy blockages, the functioning of the organs, nutritional deficiencies, and food sensitivities, among other things. We will use it to demonstrate the power of our thoughts on our muscle strength. [1]

Two people are required to do this exercise. One person will be the tester, and the other person will be the person that is being tested. The person being tested should hold his or her arm out straight to the side and resist with the arm as hard as he or she can. Once the arm is fully extended and strong with resistance, the tester should put two fingers on the wrist of the horizontally extended arm of the person being tested and apply a downward pressure on the arm for a short period of time. First, try this without saying anything (this will give a baseline). Then, after a short rest, repeat, this time saying the words, "Yes, yes, yes." Then, repeat a third time, this time saying, "No, no, no."

Most people will discover that their arm becomes weaker merely by hearing the word "no" and stronger when hearing the word "yes." It is a powerful demonstration of how the mind affects the body.

You can also self-test by touching your thumb to the middle finger of each hand to form two rings, linked through each other. Say something true—for example, "My name is [give your name]." At the same time, pull the linked fingers of the right hand against those of the left, noting the amount of pressure it takes to separate them. Then say something false—for example, "My name is [give someone else's name]." Do the same thing as before with the fingers, again noting how much pressure

---

1   Source: http://www.kinesiology.co.za/kzn/what_we_do.htm

it takes to separate the fingers. If you are like most people, you will find that your fingers easily separate when you say something false and are much stronger when you are telling the truth (you don't need to make the true and false statements aloud—silently is OK, as long as you do it each time).

How does this apply to golf and business? It will give you a simple and invisible way of testing your thinking. When you are saying negative things to yourself such as, "I always hit my ball into the water hazard," or "I just can't make cold calls," you will likely notice that your muscles are much weaker than when you are telling yourself the truth. Your body knows better than you do how harmful negative self-talk is to your performance.

One of the most stressful mind challenges people face, whether on the golf course or in my studio, is having other people watch them. This is because we all have a mental story about how we are going to perform in front of others. On the course it is very interesting to listen to people talking with each other as they are heading to the first tee, especially when paired with strangers. Many describe themselves with negative words that simply set themselves up for the way they are going to play, such as, "I'm a bad player, but I'll try not to hold you up," "I haven't played in a long time, so don't expect much," "I didn't sleep much last night," and so forth. Even though golf is simply movement with a club, we just don't seem to make up stories like that about riding a bike or playing catch with someone (even if we haven't played in a long time). Golf is one sport that seems to bring out the apologetic in us all, even before we pick up a club.

All of our thoughts are made up of words. The words that we think and use generate the energy we send out. What words do you use when you start to golf, either to yourself or to the others around you? Before you even begin your game, your words are setting the tone for your round. As the kinesiology exercise demonstrated, your words have a strong effect on your body as well as your mind. What I have learned in all my years of coaching is that there is no room for doubt. Do you really want to start your round with weak muscles?

WORDS MATTER

The words we use will generate positive or negative energy depending on how we relate to the words. Golf can be positive for some and negative for others depending on how you view the game and your previous experiences with it. Money and career are other areas where the words you use will affect your physical performance. We generate feelings through thoughts and words. However, most of the time, we are unaware that we are doing so. Part of the goal of this book is to teach you to be fully aware of how your thinking affects your performance.

Here are some examples of positive words and negative words.

Positive words	Negative words
Yes	No
I get to	I have to
I can	I will try
I have clarity	I think so

The beauty of this is that we can become aware of the words that we use and let go of the words and phrases that do not serve us. Thinking positive thoughts and using positive words will send out a whole new energy toward what you wish to achieve. It is the reason why if you want to laugh, you can begin to fake a laugh and make your laugh real for a very short period of time. At the same time, you can get your mind and body ready to perform before you perform. Many top performers do this whether they know it or not. I can tell you for myself that when I have a clear outcome of what I would like to achieve before I start, I produce great results. I not only see this happening, but I can feel it as well. It is not always easy to describe, but I am certainly not alone.

Many of the great performers in their line of work do this much of the time without even knowing. In a conversation I had with former Minnesota North Stars goalie Don Beaupre, I asked him how he prepared for games when he played in the NHL. You could tell that his passion level kicked up a notch as he explained how he could play a game in his mind before playing the actual game. And oftentimes he made similar saves in the game.

I recommend closely watching the words that you use for the next month and writing down all the positive and negative words that stand out to you in any given day. You may wish to ask those who know you really well to help you become aware of how you use different words. Of course, at the beginning, this might drive you a little crazy, but it is an awareness that can help you make a difference. Try playing a round of golf with a very good and understanding friend who has agreed to point out to you when you make a negative statement. Take just a minute to change that statement and then note how your body almost immediately feels stronger and more confident. Then, take a moment and test your muscles before and after the statement. Do this during your workday as well and note the results you achieve when you speak more positively to yourself. Your words are perhaps your most powerful tool in life. They are a good reflection of what energy you are sending out when seeking to achieve your target.

RELAXING MUSCLE TENSION

Do you feel yourself tensing up before an important meeting or presentation? Is your entire body tense when you approach the first tee? When faced with implementing an important new business initiative, do you find yourself getting nervous about whether or not you can pull it off? When top performance is required, do you relish the challenge or feel like the world is caving in on top of you?

Tension is a huge factor in making mistakes in your golf swing. Unlike most other sports, the harder you swing at the golf ball in an attempt to hit it farther, the shorter it will go. Gripping the club too hard can cause the clubface to close or open at impact. Tight muscles in the shoulders can restrict you from completing your backswing, while the "yips" in putting and chipping are usually a result of involuntary tightening of the affected muscles.

Why does this happen? Confusion—or, the word we like to use, interference. Interference can be internal with our own minds or external with our environments. In business, tension results in tight, sore shoulders, shaking hands, and even weak speech. Do you know where tension is held in your body? Do you have a technique to instantly release it?

> *"The voice, like the face, expresses rather accurately what is in the mind. It is evident that we are born with the instinctive ability to use the voice easily and freely without any expression, without any instruction. This, of course cannot be considered high art, but at least it has something to do with good free tone quality. Why, then, do we not all sing with good tone quality? Almost any singer will agree that muscular tension is the main cause of our bad tones." (Citation: 1944 Harvard Dictionary of Music)*

One of my clients, Kathryn, taught me a technique she teaches her students in intuitive studies. Because this technique quiets the mental chatter of the brain, she uses it as a quick way to enter into a light focus state (also known as a trance). While we certainly don't need to enter in a trance when we golf or do business, we often do need to go into our relaxed, yet high-performing mode that can be subconscious. This technique also allows for almost instantaneous relaxation of tension.

Kathryn told me that the quickest way to enter into this state of relaxation is by focusing on and then relaxing your tongue. When we talk to ourselves (which we do constantly), we tend to move our tongues, just as if we were verbalizing out loud. If you concentrate on relaxing your tongue, you make it almost impossible for this subvocalization to occur.

When you reduce your mental ruminating, you release the tension you carry in your jaw.

Each person must find his or her own best way of relaxing his or her tongue. Kathryn suggests you imagine your tongue floating in your mouth while letting your chin drop slightly and your jaw loosen. Of course, don't forget to breathe. Most of us hold our breath when we are tense. I have watched golfers hold their breath during almost every swing. Remember that inhaling stimulates and exhaling relaxes, so spend a little longer exhaling than you do inhaling. However, each should be at least five seconds long.

Once you have mastered this technique, you can loosen your tongue in a matter of seconds. This exercise puts you into a very mild relaxed state in which your brainwaves are altered from high speed beta waves to a slower alpha state. Sometimes it helps to keep powerful images in your mind of what you want to achieve or positive memories of the past. Try doing this on the tee, before your drive, or right before you sink a putt. See if it helps reduce your mental chatter and increase your focus on your target.

Of course, tongue loosening will not work for everyone. If it doesn't work for you, there are other simple muscle relaxation techniques that can be done anywhere, including on the course, at your desk, or in your client's office. Just parting your lips will provide some relief because we all carry so much tension in our jaws.

Another common tension relaxer is to distract yourself from mental stress by drawing a figure eight into your palm with your finger. Try it and see how quickly it works. You can also pinch your ear lobes between your thumb and index finger. Hold the lobes with a firm grip while allowing the weight of your arms to pull your ears down. If you are holding lots of tension in this area, you will notice instant relief as pressure is released from your head, your neck, and your shoulders.

No matter what you are doing, whether it is swinging a club or calling on a customer, the optimum results will come from a relaxed body and a focused mind. We will discuss focus in the next chapter.

Chapter Six

Mapping Your Strategy

The architect of a golf course designs the layout of each hole so that it has obstacles and hazards. These obstacles and hazards are meant to defend the course. Grasses (long and short), plants, trees, forests, the contour of the land (flat, undulating, or elevated), sand traps, and moats (either dry ditches or filled with water) are strategically placed to intimidate and challenge you. Meanwhile, the golfer is attacking the course. The architect wants to make sure you know there is a price to pay for trying to conquer each hole.

Your job is to find the easiest route to the pin that will result in the fewest number of strokes being taken. You can play aggressively or play it safe, with both routes having advantages and disadvantages. You choose which club to use, depending on which way you plan on attacking the hole. You have the choice to go directly through bunkers or over the water, or you can decide to go around them. The bunkers, water hazards, and other obstacles are put there to distract you. If you focus on the distractions you will inevitably find yourself inside a sand trap or lost in a water hole. The ball never lies. It goes where you hit it, and you hit it toward what you focus upon. In some instances, it may hit some things that you least expected—a bird, sprinkler head, person, etc. Mapping your strategy means you plan your hole in advance, deciding on the best club for your attack, determining your ability to hit a certain distance, and then focusing on the target instead of on the obstacles.

In your business and professional life, you also face the same challenges. When encountering potential hazards or obstacles, you may have to decide "How can we be more aggressive in this situation? How can we best attack? What obstacles are easiest to hurdle? What tools do I use in this situation?" At other times it could be more prudent to ask, "Is this a time to play it safe and regroup? What strengths can we build on to embrace the situation as an opportunity to remain clear on our clients' needs while being aware of the competition? How can we build on the advantages we already have?"

In the game of golf and in the game of business, you get to have a strategy in mind before you pick up a club, call a client, or open a file. You get to have a clear target in mind and have knowledge and awareness of the course or situation. You get to be familiar with the tools you will be using and the obstacles along the way. No professional golfer would ever play a hole without knowing what they would like to do beforehand. No successful businessperson would call on a client without thoroughly researching the client's business. Mapping your strategy is your plan for success.

Golf is a sport that has an 85 to 90 percent failure rate, even at a professional level. The thing to ask yourself is, "In the midst of failing, can I see the possibilities? Even while dealing with the inevitable letdowns, can I keep my mind on the target?" In any business, you will also encounter a high degree of failure. You will not land every client or nail every presentation. As is the case with the best golfers, the best businesspeople are able to see the possibilities in every failure and stay focused on their goals and target.

Effective CEOs coach their teams to be able to cope with obstacles and handle failures so they can enhance the performance of their company. It is not a surprise that golf is the sport played by more CEOs than any other game. Learning the strategy of golf will aid anyone with the strategy of business. Imagine being a team leader who uses golf as a training tool and learning ground rather than merely playing golf as a game. By learning the methods we teach, you will start to ask yourself, "What did I learn today? What new insights did I discover, and how could I apply them to my team and business performance?"

In this chapter, we will be discussing the strategy of the game of golf as well as the playing of the "game" of business. As we have discussed, most people skip the critical steps we have laid out in previous chapters. They walk up to the first hole with no strategy, plan, or target. In the same way, most businesspeople start each day without a plan, perhaps even being proud of their ability to "shoot from the hip." The critical elements to playing golf are to have a strategy and a target, learn to focus on that target, and then keep score to know how you are doing when it comes to accomplishing your goals. I will discuss each of these in some depth while pointing out the similarities to business strategy.

It is very hard to get to the next level in business or in golf by simply keeping your strategy in your head. Have you laid out what you wish to achieve and what your goals are for the coming year? On the course, do you know where you are headed, and do you have a clear idea of how to approach it? Does everyone in your business know the process you are using and why? Is everyone executing the required procedures uniformly? When you decide to commit to a process and stay with it, you will enhance your abilities, reduce the interference, and improve your efficiency while increasing the bottom line. On the course you will simply see how you can play the game from a broader perspective that will allow you to deal with any interference faster and easier.

By mapping your strategy, you will begin to see new ways in which you can open up to the possibilities. This will help you clearly identify, document, understand, and follow your goals and plans to a desired outcome.

The most successful leaders are the ones who execute their plans well. They know how to bring focus and accountability to their organizations. The most successful golfers are ones who accept coaching from themselves and others on a regular basis. They hold themselves accountable for their games.

Over my years working as a golf professional at many different country clubs, resorts, etc., around the United States, I played with members from time to time. Many of these members were business owners and CEOs from some of the top companies in the country. It would blow my mind how they would choose to play the game. Sometimes they would look down the fairway at what they thought was the target, but in reality they never really had a target. They looked in a general area for where to hit the ball, focused on their technique, such as their stance or swing, and then completely lost the target, hitting the ball in the general direction of forward. For many, no one had ever told them to pick a specific target, hold it in mind, and aim for it.

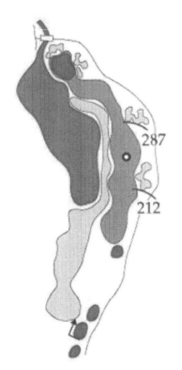

Many powerful business people do the exact same thing in their businesses. I have often wondered how they could run their company with that kind of mindset. In business, companies have goals that can be lost in the day-to-day interference that occurs. Instead of figuring out how to get around these obstacles, many people get stuck. I often advise my clients to play the hole backward as a strategy in both golf and business. The ability to look at the pathway to success backward allows one to see different ways of avoiding obstacles and dealing with interference, just like playing the course backward. We do so by breaking the path down into smaller steps that are achievable so that the overall goal is not overwhelming. Setting small, intermediary targets allows one to reach his or her expectations and makes the pathway to success more enjoyable.

MAPPING THE COURSE EXERCISE

Mapping the course allows you to free yourself from thinking about the "right way" to play the course and encourages you to look at the course with fresh eyes. Playing the hole backward lets you see the many possibilities for reaching your target. The following pictures are examples of how you can look at the course and see that there are several different ways to achieve your desired outcome. We laid this out to show you that even if your original intent to play the hole does not work, it does not mean that you can't achieve your outcome.

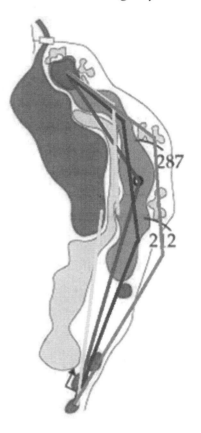

Here is the hole you will map—a 412-yard par-four. Mark three different ways in which you see being able to achieve your target score.

Look at this hole and create a strategy for how you would play it, starting at the tee box and mapping out four strokes (for a par). What is your target for your first shot? Second? Third?

VARIOUS WAYS OF PLAYING THIS HOLE

After you have drawn out your strategy, notice the four different strategies that I have created. There are, of course, an endless number of ways to play this (and every) hole.

By seeing the bigger picture, you can define the possibilities.

Here are four pathways you can follow by example in order to achieve a score of par at this hole. However, it is important to play your own game and use your natural abilities. If you are the red golfer in the image, you hit the ball down the middle of the fairway with a beautiful drive, made it onto the green on your second shot, and then two-putted the ball into the hole. If you are the blue golfer, it took you three shots to get the ball on the green, but you one-putted. If you're the yellow golfer, you missed your drive and hit the ball into the water, taking a penalty. Your next shot, though, went onto the green, and then you chipped the ball in the hole from the fairway without putting. If you're the orange golfer, you missed your drive way right, hitting the ball out of bounds. Your second shot went into the sand trap, but you recovered onto the green in three shots and one-putted. Despite all the different ways this hole was played by the four golfers, they all scored par.

When we stand at the tee box getting ready to hit our first shot, we don't often think of the options we have to get the ball into the hole with the least amount of shots. Most golfers just pick up the club and whack it as hard as possible in the general direction of the hole. As you can see from this exercise, even a terrible drive, landing in interference or three-putting can still give you a good result on the hole if you have a strategy.

Perhaps making par on this hole is not within your skill level in golf. For example, you might currently shoot an average of one hundred, but your goal is to score eighty-five on this golf course for the day. A round in which you par every hole would give you a score of seventy-two. So, if your goal is to shoot eighty-five, you could have thirteen holes in which you scored a bogey (one-over par). The other five holes you would have to make a par. This particular hole is ranked by handicap as the fifth hardest hole on the course, and you might decide that shooting a bogey is more attainable for you on this hole. Thus, your strategy would change to add an additional stroke. When you map your overall strategy for the game, you can plan which holes you will par and which you will bogey (or double bogey, depending on your skill level). You won't, of course, always hit your goal, but you are far more likely to do so with a strategy.

By creating a concrete plan for achieving your desired score in golf, you are much more likely to stick to that plan. The golf hole can be overwhelming until broken down into strokes. By breaking it down into increments, you can see how you can easily hit your ball in a way to ultimately achieve success.

MAPPING YOUR FAVORITE COURSE

A fun exercise to learn more about your abilities is to get the course map from your favorite golf course. Almost all golf courses will have a map of their holes available for you online. Of course, all golf courses hand out a small map with your score card. But, this is an exercise that takes some time and is done well in advance.

You can map out each hole just as we did in the exercise above. Visualize yourself making each shot. Ask yourself which club you would use. Perhaps imagine who you are playing with, what the weather is like, and even what you are wearing. Visualization is a powerful technique for improving your golf game and beginning to live into your dreams.

There is a famous story about a Major, James Nesmeth, who spent seven years as a prisoner of war in North Vietnam. During those seven years, he was imprisoned in a cage that was approximately four-and-a-half feet high and five feet long. To keep himself sane, he came up with an amazing visualization technique. During almost the entire time he was imprisoned, he saw no one, talked to no one, and experienced no physical activity. During the first few months, he did almost nothing but hope and pray for his release. Then he realized he had to find some way to occupy his life. That's when he learned to visualize.

In his mind, he selected his favorite golf course and started playing golf. Every day, he played a full eighteen holes at this course, taking exactly as long to visualize the game as it would have taken him to play it in real life. He experienced everything to the last detail. He saw himself dressed in his golfing clothes and visualized his partners. He smelled the fragrance of the grass and the scent of the trees. Sometimes he would visualize different weather conditions, from bright sunny days to windy overcast weather. He had all the time in the world, so he would visualize every detail—how long it took to walk between holes, the scampering of small animals, and the sounds of the birds.

In his visualization he could feel the grip of the club in his hands and the feel the swing in his arms. He would see the ball fly and land exactly where he had planned it to land. He visualized himself playing perfectly. No missed shots or muffed putts.

Before his imprisonment, James had been an average weekend golfer, shooting in the mid to low nineties. After his involuntary break from the game, he went out for the first time and shot a seventy-four! Despite the harsh physical conditions of his imprisonment and not touching a club for seven years, he had shaved twenty strokes off his average score.

Of course, in real life we don't have the time to visualize playing eighteen holes of golf every day. But, we can plan out our strategy and, while doing so, visualize us playing those holes perfectly.

Mapping your strategy and visualization are also very important tools for business. You will, of course, want to learn as much about your customers as you can before calling on them. If you can, perhaps you might be able to find the layout of their office. Then, visualize your call. What do you say? What are you wearing? Where do you sit? How does the customer respond to your pitch? Think of how you can "imprint the target" in your business. Choose an area in which you'd like to improve, and visualize specifically how success would look in that area. What image do you see in your mind's eye? What do you need to do to get there? Do you actually believe you can achieve it? Exercises like club throwing remind us of the power of a precise target. Instead of staying stuck in the how, we can trust more in the innate tools we already have. By focusing on the target and relaxing, we can gain confidence and increase performance in everything we do.

An example more of us can relate to is from Tony. Tony told me that a stressful part of his life was his weekend commute up in northern Minnesota. He left the office tired and anxious to get to the lake with his family for their Friday afternoon commute, only to spend the next three hours frustrated and upset about the traffic and his family's dawdling. Every Friday night he arrived at his cabin exhausted and cranky, only to repeat the process two days later. I asked him to write out five different ways to get to his cabin.

Being a practical man, Tony pulled out a map and discovered there were, in fact, five different routes he could take to the cabin. He decided to start taking a different route that was slower but more enjoyable and less stressful. He also realized he could leave an hour later and avoid some of the traffic. This way Tony could not only enjoy the process of getting to his cabin, he could start to enjoy the whole weekend as soon as he got in his car. By mapping out his strategy in advance, Tony cut down on the stress in his life and began to enjoy the things he was supposed to.

Chapter Seven

Aiming for the Target

Most people playing golf think that they have a target. I can tell you from my experience as a golf professional, however, that for many people the target is not truly imprinted in the mind through impact. The tendency is to work on the swing, even when you think you have a target. Aiming in the general destination of the hole, is not the target. In the same way, a business person will often work extremely hard, making many calls, for example, without truly having a plan, strategy, or target in mind. From my experience it is much easier to make a difference when people are clear on their intention. In golf when you are thinking in front of the ball instead of behind the ball you will be clear. Example most people think of grip stance and swing, which is all behind the ball. Thus there is no target.

The best players and organizations see their paths clearly and yet are constantly refining them. However, most golfers and business owners do not understand how powerful sustaining a clear target can be. When applied correctly, it will work like magic, resulting in lower scores on the course and higher profitability for the business.

For everyone that I have talked to the hole is the smallest target when we first look at the three different objects. Yet the clay pigeon and the liner fit inside of the hole. This leads to just one of the opportunities for us to focus on a target and let go of the interference. The target is not just the hole; it is a very small part of the hole.

People often think they can improve their putting by practicing how they putt. They focus on their stance, how they hold the club, how they position the club to the ball, and so on. In business, a salesperson may spend countless hours studying sales training techniques and devoting days to learning all about the features and benefits of the product he or she is going to sell. In both situations, people focus on the mechanics, which are needed in some cases, but lose track of the target at the same time.

Without a doubt, one of the primary causes of a slump in any business or golf/sports performance is fear, apprehension, insecurity, or indecision. Concentration is based on our thought patterns. Our bodies and their muscle movements center on the signals from our minds. If the mind is focused on fear or insecurity, our bodies will not perform at an optimal level.

The key to improving performance in anything is to always keep the target in mind. Keeping the target in mind shifts the focus from technique to the goal. In golf it is knowing how you want the ball to travel through the air or roll into the cup—right-center, left-center, middle. In business, the more you focus on how you want the customer to respond and meeting the customer's needs, the more likely you are to close a sale.

The finger next to the hole allows for people to imprint the target while performing.

It's about changing mindset. If you spend too much time worrying about the mechanics of the perfect shot or putting stroke (keeping your arms straight, bringing the putter back smoothly, making sure you follow through on the stroke), then you begin thinking about everything but the real target. Far too many golfers will change how they putt but not see any improvement in their scores. Sometimes they simply stop playing golf because their game has become too embarrassing or they believe they don't have enough time to practice (which is not necessarily a reality). What they don't realize is that they have been playing without a target.

Most professionals, when looking at their businesses, often find the same thing to be true. They too are
playing without a clear target. In general people do not
change the way they think until they have to or until it
is forced upon them. Why change if things are work-
ing fine? Why fix it if it isn't broken? The answer is that change is moving
faster today than ever before, so the ability to accept and embrace change
is critical.

The good news is that you can change the way you think any time you
want. You can change your perception before you are forced into it and
before an emergency occurs or you give up golf out of frustration. You can
change your way of thinking now, and doing so could change your business
and life for the better.

While there are many things that can get in our way of seeing the target,
the biggest obstacle is our mindset of what works and doesn't work. Our
preconceived ideas of how things should be done can become our biggest
roadblocks to success. Don Beaupre started his business Beaupre Aerial (a
lift rental and repair company) in 2003. Like many companies, they wanted
to improve the bottom line and enhance communication between staff and
clients. In 2009, Don found pricing was becoming a struggle, as many of his
clients were looking for discounting in a tough economy. Don was skeptical
that he and his business partner, John, could fix the business without any help.
Don and John came into the studio looking for new insights for themselves
and their team. Don knew the value of coaching in regards to sports teams
but was unsure of the effectiveness of business coaching.

Don found that, instead of focusing on changing pricing (as they had
been discussing), what he and his company needed were new techniques
for determining and focusing on the client's needs, as well as finding new
clients. This is similar to the putting exercise, where pricing is the regular
way of putting, and new techniques are putting with eyes closed, one-
handed, and eyes on the target. Don and John learned how, through the
putting and other exercises, to change their focus and how to enjoy the
process of doing so.

After going through these exercises, the staff of Beaupre Aerial learned to listen more carefully to their clients and implement new strategies for providing services that met their needs. However, if the clients asked for too much, Don and his company realized they needed to remain clear on what they offered to existing clients. They were selling good products with great service and did not need to completely change what they had been doing in order to stay alive. At the same time, it was also a possibility to find new clients. This has significantly increased the company's bottom line. Along with better external communication with outsiders, such as customers, Beaupre Aerial also learned to communicate better internally. This helped employees understand company goals and work toward common targets.

As Don stated, "At first, I didn't realize how much the concepts Dan taught applied to me. They worked so well that this past year we enrolled our executive and management teams back into the program. By focusing on a common target we gained over ninety new clients within two months of beginning the program in a difficult economy. While in the recession, we needed to focus on a new client base that was less price-sensitive. We have all discovered new possibilities. We're communicating better both internally and externally while enjoying working together more than ever."

Because Don liked to golf, he also set a goal that year to shoot four rounds in the seventies (he was previously shooting in the eighties). The result? After playing his first five rounds that year, Don shot four rounds in the seventies, achieving his goal within two months. The change of mindset was critical. He did not devote any more time to practicing but still saw considerable improvement in his game.

WHAT IS YOUR TARGET?

In golf and in business, a critical step that most people miss is to clearly define their target. The target is the hole, not the golf ball. It is similar to shooting baskets in basketball, where the hoop is the target, not the basketball. Or think of throwing wadded up paper into a wastebasket across the room. The wastebasket is the target, not the paper. Once people define what the target is, which isn't always as easy as it sounds, they can then learn how best to focus on the target, rather than on the distractions around them.

How do we see size, color, shape, distance, speed, and depth? It has to do with our previous experience, environment, training, and development. Perception is a learned skill. Backgrounds, surroundings, objects, mood, weather, and a host of other factors all influence and affect our ability to look, see, and act. Why do objects seem to be farther away, closer, larger, or smaller? Why do straight lines sometimes seem to appear to be crooked and lines of the same length seem to be longer or shorter? It is the power of our focus and the awareness of the target.

IMPRINTING THE TARGET

Most golfers, especially when they start playing, have only a general idea where they want to hit the ball before they swing (for example, down the fairway or toward the green). This is precisely where the ball goes—in the general direction—which is usually not the intended line of flight.

As golfers progress, they typically pick more specific targets, such as shooting at the pin on a specific green. Yet even shooting at the pin is a general direction. Do you really want the ball to hit the flagstick on the fly, or do you want it to land directly in the cup? Perhaps where you want the ball to land is six feet in front of the cup and roll in (or six feet behind the cup if you have backspin). Golfers hesitate to pick a specific target because of fear of failure. In other words, if they aim for a target and miss, they think they've failed. Or perhaps is it simply that they don't believe that they can

When we maintain a clear image of the target throughout the
Performance it is much easier to achieve.

Mark a former national trap shooter came to me seeking to learn how to play golf. He was in his 60's and wanted to spend time on the link when retired. He was scoring in the in the upper 90's at the time and a fairly new golfer. His goal was to score in the 70's. Within 3 weeks Mark had scored a 77, by far his all time low, but not a surprise. Mark already knew how to focus on a target and let go of interference. He could shoot a 100 plus clay pigeons in a row. He already knew how to focus on a target, but never knew how to do that with golf until we dialed in on the target when hitting golf balls. Mark swing had changed very rapidly and he became very precise. The coaching process had allowed Mark to find his our authentic game. I was also able to share with him the target (golf hole) was the same size as the clay pigeon that he was used to shooting in the pasted.

The same thing often happens in business. People choose a general direction (such as an increase in sales) instead of setting a clearly defined goal (a dollar amount increase). Often, people pick a general target so they don't feel badly about failing if they miss it. By doing so, they also have no clear measurement of the success of their effort. It is like playing golf without keeping score, and therefore never really knowing if you are improving your game.

Professional golfers know that golf balls don't lie. If the ball goes short or long, right or left, high or low, there's a reason for it. There's no mystery to a bad shot—your mind simply wasn't on the target. Yes, there are always many things that are out of our control (like a shot bouncing off of a sprinkler head and into a hazard), but, in general, when the ball floats off line of our target, it is a sign that we lost the target through impact.

The idea of focusing on the target and visualizing it in your mind is called "imprinting the target." First, you choose a specific target. For a golfer it could be a spot ten feet in front of the red flag on top of the yellow pin if hitting an approach shot onto a green. Keep the image of the target in your mind, whether it is as you address the ball as a golfer or whether you are in a sales meeting. If you can keep the image of the target in your mind through impact—either by hitting a golf ball or through the meeting at work—you've imprinted the target. In other words, your physical eyes will see what's in front of you (the ball on the ground or the person with whom you are meeting), but in your mind's eye you will see the target. For some reason it is much easier to do in other activities, like riding a bike, for example. We do not look down at our feet but instead on the road or path ahead of us. There is no conscious thought of how to properly pedal or how much pressure to use with our legs; we simply look ahead and go.

A good coach knows that if he or she can get clients to stop focusing on the mechanics of the swing and start focusing on the target while keeping focus through impact, the player will produce extraordinary shots. Several years ago I was working with a CEO who was having a difficult time understanding this concept until I related it to his business.

I asked him what would happen if all he did was train his salespeople but never let them go out to sell anything. The answer is that the business would fail and all of the work would go to waste. In golf there are many great players when it comes to the driving range, but they don't know how to transfer their game to the course. When trying to make this transfer, they should allow themselves to change the way they practice. It is crucial to have the same mindset on the range as you do on the course, which generates familiarity and confidence when you are actually playing the game.

When putting, you can actually go one step further by imprinting the target (the cup) and then seeing the result you want to take place before you swing. Years ago I conducted a study where I told a group of people to visualize the golf ball dropping into the hole before they made the putt. This group was 10 percent more accurate than those who did not visualize the putt going in. While 10 percent may not seem like much at first glance, if the average golfer takes two putts per hole, that's thirty-six strokes in eighteen holes. Sinking 10 percent more putts would shave four strokes per round by doing nothing more than visualizing the putt going in the hole before making the putt. What effect could a 10 percent increase in sales have in your business?

The orange ball is used to help individuals find a clear focus on a target.

As a golf coach, I recognized early on that many people didn't imprint the target when looking at the hole. The hole seems to be too generic for many golfers, often blending in with the background. Hold this image five feet away from you. Look at the balls. Now focus on the colored ball. Notice how it stands out and the others fade into the background. This is an example of imprinting the target.

IMPRINTING YOUR TARGET IN BUSINESS

Just as imprinting your target in golf can make a huge difference in your game, imprinting your target in business can enhance your business performance. Take a moment now to think of how you can "imprint the target" in your business. Choose an area in which you'd like to see improvement, and visualize specifically how success would look in that area. What images do you see in your mind's eye, and what do you need to do to get there? Do you actually believe you can achieve it? For example, perhaps when you think of success in your business, you imagine yourself in a plush corner office, relaxed while talking to a customer who is eager to hire you. Imprint that feeling into your body and mind until it feels as natural to you as throwing a club toward a target. Do not let the process of how you will do it get in the way. By imprinting your goal or target and the feeling you have when experiencing that goal.

Look at the hole as though you were going to play the hole in your mind. If the goal is to get the ball next to the pin or in the hole, what color is the pin? Where do you see the pin in relationship to the hole? How high do you want the ball to travel? How many bounces when it lands on the green? This would all be part of you imprinting the target in your mind before you choose to play. The picture that you paint in your mind must be (or gets to be) clear to what you want to achieve. Commit to the target and trust the shot, learn what happened and let go so you can enjoy the moment.

Chapter Eight

Playing the Game

Finally you are ready to go out and play the game. The purpose of this chapter is not to give you golf lessons but rather to give you awareness to the most important things to keep in mind before, during, and after a round of golf regarding your mental game.

Play can mean powerful learning about yourself. It is certainly our choice to reflect and understand what this means to get the most out of your ability. The play of the game can get lost in a hurry when we don't play to our best potential. Our greatness comes from a positive view of our inconsistency of one's experience. Being inconsistent is a given with golf. So being inconsistent can be embraced, so you can learn from the let down.

PLAYING YOUR OWN GAME: WHAT YOU'D LIKE TO GET OUT OF THE EXPERIENCE

For many of us, we tend to wake up thinking of what we need to get done within the day. From time to time, our thoughts may go into what we should have done yesterday, last week, or any time before then. When I coach golfers, one of the first questions I ask is why they play. It is amazing that, for many, that question is difficult to answer. The direct question has never been asked to them, and yet some of these people have belonged to several country clubs for the majority of their lives.

There may be many reasons why we play golf; in fact, there may be as many reasons as there are us. It is easy to get caught up in other people's games and not allow ourselves to stay focused on our own game. Understanding how to play your own game is one of the biggest components to achieving your peak performance and getting what you want out of the experience. Perhaps you play because you enjoy being outdoors, or maybe you are seeking to perform or challenge yourself, compete with others, or spend time with family and friends. When someone calls you and asks if you want to play nine holes, you say, "Sure, that sounds like fun," but what is in it for you that day? How are you choosing to describe the fun? If we don't know what we want out of the experience before we begin, it can be really hard to determine what to do when things aren't working out the way we planned. In some cases a mini breakdown may appear if the performance is not working to your liking. If so, you need to add this step to your game plan. What are you going to do if you don't perform well?

Several years ago my wife and I traveled to Arizona for a New Year's getaway. We stayed at a resort with a golf course on site. It was a beautiful course and a great way to kick off New Year's Eve Day. We were planning on playing the round of golf by ourselves. She was fairly new to the game at the time and felt a bit intimidated about playing golf with others. We hit balls at the range for a few minutes and then built up our confidence by making a few putts at the nearby putting green. At this point we were very relaxed and had a few minutes to spare before our tee time.

There was an outdoor fire pit near the putting green, and we sat around the fire and shared what each of us would like to get out of our upcoming golf experience. We discussed our time hitting the ball and the non-performance time as well. We also talked about what we would do if either of us seemed to be breaking down. How would we coach one another to achieve peak performance? We felt clear about the conversation by the time it was our turn to head to the first tee and play the game.

However, the game we had planned had changed by the time we went to the first tee. We learned that we were now going to be paired with another twosome. I could see my wife's face turn pale, but there wasn't a whole lot we could do since the course had paired us up to play with others. (We certainly could have elected to not play that day, but we decided to go ahead.)

The other twosome appeared to be a father-son combination. The kid was in his younger teens and was so skinny that he could wrap his belt around his waist a couple of times. Then he stepped up to the tee and hit the ball over three hundred yards. The father noticed that my shirt had a logo of my old business, Better Golf. These two things soon changed my expectations of the game as well. I felt a pressure to play well, and instead my tee shot went at least sixty yards short of his drive and slightly off to the right. I could feel that I wasn't in the game, and my wife could see the same thing as well. There was no flow in my swing, tension crept into my body, and it was clear that I had forgotten the game that I was choosing to play.

My wife had her breakdown before she even got to her tee box, but she did just fine by becoming aware of how the game changed and what she would now like to get out of the experience. The kid had put his ball on the green in two shots, and it took me three good shots to get on the green. We both ended up with a par five. It is interesting to ask why I even cared what he did or scored. On the second hole, the father called me by the wrong name (Doug rather than Dan) before I teed off. For some reason that caused me to realize that no one really cared about how I played. I stepped up to tee off on a par three, hit the ball, and it went flying, hit the flag stick, and dropped down next to the hole. As I walked back to the cart, I could hear the son tell his father that my name was Dan. I laughed and said, "I think I will play by the name Doug today; he golfs better," and we all laughed. This story illustrates how quickly we can lose our own game if we allow interference to take over and how quickly relaxing and focusing on the joy of the game can help us regain it.

I suggest that you come up with something to focus on for the round that allows you to understand the value that the game can provide. If you were to go out and play a round and you scored a ninety, and it took you ten seconds to hit each shot—that means grab the club, set up, and hit the ball—that is fifteen minutes' worth of ball-hitting time (90 x 10 seconds = 900 seconds = 15 minutes). An average eighteen-hole round of golf takes us four hours to play. If you're only hitting the ball for fifteen minutes, what are you doing with the other three hours and forty five minutes?

This thought process is very important to keep in your mind, especially when on the first tee when others are standing around and waiting for you to hit the shot. What are you thinking and doing that will allow yourself to remain focused on your desired outcomes throughout your experience?

The question we often use at Performance In Motion is, "What did you learn today?" versus "How well did you do?" Because, even if you decide not to keep score, you can still challenge yourself on whether you were able to stay clear on what you wanted out of the experience.

One to three days after your round, allow yourself to reflect on what you achieved. Were you able to stay focused on the ball for all fifteen minutes of ball-hitting time? What did you choose to do when you weren't hitting the ball? Were you able to achieve what you set out to do, or did distractions and interference get in the way? Answering these questions about your experience will help you become more aware of how to make changes in the future. Even if things do not turn out the way you would have liked, there is always an opportunity to understand why it happened and to determine what you can do next time to improve your performance and get more enjoyment out of the experience.

STRATEGIZE EACH HOLE

As we have mentioned, it's helpful to know what your game plan is before you even play. How are you choosing to play your own game with your own abilities? As mentioned earlier in this book, we talked about mapping out a hole to help you strategize and understand the possibilities. It could be a course that you play frequently or one that you look up on the Internet before you play. If it is a course you've seen before, go through the scorecard or virtual tour online to see where you could take advantage of the course and achieve your desired outcomes. If there is a hole where you always seem to take a six, take a closer look and determine how you could score lower while still playing within your abilities.

If it is a course you have not seen before, go through the scorecard and virtual tour online and map out each hole to see the possibilities of what you could achieve. Develop a realistic idea of what your score could be for the course and set a target.

It is also important to realize that you may miss certain shots on the course, but you can still recover from those you did not execute to your liking. When you look at the course and map it out, we suggest that you do this in several different ways so you can not only define the best path to your target but also understand the possibilities for recovering from shots that you did not hit as planned.

Another aspect of strategizing that commonly helps people is breaking up the game three holes at a time. This can be done when playing either nine or eighteen holes. This helps because the game can be somewhat overwhelming and distracting, especially when you are constantly thinking about your score. By breaking up the game into three-hole sections, you allow yourself to refocus and frequently look at a new game within the game. This will help you stay alert rather than zone out if you realize your first three holes did not go as planned.

PERMISSION TO SCORE LOW

How many times have you been scoring one of your career rounds only to have a major breakdown on the final few holes? This often happens to golfers of any ability when they are unprepared and haven't given themselves permission to score low or win a particular game or match.

Take, for example, a couple of different scenarios on the professional level. Tom Watson, at age fifty-nine, was leading the British Open for three consecutive rounds and literally played seventeen-and-a-half great holes in his final regulation round, only to find himself over the green on his second shot on the par-four eighteenth hole. He simply needed to get up and down in order to win the tournament, but during the next two shots, he looked as though he lost the target. He ended up in a playoff. In the playoff, the announcers even mentioned that he looked tired—and he did look tired— but did he actually give himself permission to win the tournament? At his age it would have been an unprecedented accomplishment, likely putting doubt into his mind as to if it was possible (which seemed to be the case).

Another example is Rory McIlroy. Leading the 2011 Masters through three rounds, he had a breakdown on the back nine in the fourth round and fell out of contention quickly. The game shows us just how humbling golf and life can be. When we are not clear on our abilities to succeed, we will often find ways to prevent success from happening.

Before you set out to do a task or play a game, write a paragraph affirming how you have achieved your desired success. This can be done weeks or months ahead of time. While it is important to accept permission from yourself, you should also accept it from others, including family, friends, peers, and leaders.

The inner boardroom is a part of conversations I have with many clients. It is the group of voices we have in our heads that tell us we can or cannot do something (these may be attached to certain people, such as a mom, dad, friend, coworker, etc.). The voices can often hold us back from achieving what we can and what we deserve. Recognizing these voices allows us to make the necessary changes to give ourselves permission to score low and win.

AWARENESS OF YOUR THOUGHT PROCESS

The first step to any game is to realize that you are in one. However, for many people, the first tee can be a frightening experience. It is often the only place on the course where others may be gathered around to watch you tee off. It is critical to be aware of the interference in situations like these (in this case, the people) and redirect your thought process to your intended target. This is easier said than done, and we can find ourselves distracted by a number of things that take our focus away.

If you notice yourself losing the target or hitting a number of undesired shots in a row, you first need to ask yourself why. Are you keeping the target through impact, or are you lining up your shot and then focusing on how to hit the ball? The mind can drift in many different directions in a very short period of time. Even when we look at a target, without a conscious thought to hold the target through impact, the ball can easily go off course. It is important to recognize that there is no fixing your swing if you losted your target, however golfers tend to do this all the time. If you were walking on a side walk to get into some ones house and tripped, you wouldn't declare your style of walking bad and try and fix your walking, rather you may simple blame the awareness of what you didn't see on the side walk and keep moving.

THE AWARENESS OF WHAT YOU ARE THINKING AND FEELING

When connecting with the club and ball, it is also important to understand the connection to the target. It is a feeling that can be described as an awareness of the club and the ball (see illustration below). The minus is when we hit behind the ball, and the plus is when we hit on top of the ball. The turf is taken after the shot when the ball is hit solidly at the target. This is a zero, a great feeling of solid contact with the club and the ball.

Connecting to the Target
What does the club and the ball feel like when hitting the ball

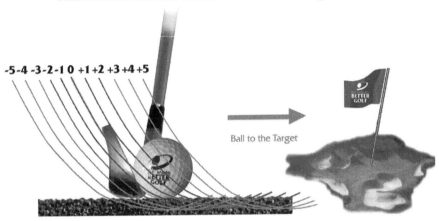

The plus and minus helps an individual become aware of their contact with the ball as they focus on the target.

DEALING WITH FRUSTRATION

Frustration is another reason why we lose focus on the target. One of the main causes of our anger is that when we hit a bad shot or two, we are afraid we will do it again. It is not so much the anger of missing the target in the first place but the fear of continuing to do it for an extended period of time. If I knew I would start my round with two double-bogeys but end up with seven birdies and the rest pars to score a sixty-nine, I would be happy. However, after those first two bogeys, there is no way of knowing that I will break through and play great for sixteen holes to end the round. Being aware of the possibility of a breakthrough can reduce frustration and bring your mind back to the task at hand more quickly.

What are the thoughts that allow a breakthrough? Keep saying to yourself, "Yes, yes, yes" (encouragement); "In, in, in" (as the ball goes in the hole); and "Allow, allow, allow" (allowing yourself to achieve a particular shot). Simply repeating words like these can have a significant effect on the way in which you choose to play your game.

Over the years, I have followed a number of people who have had outdated beliefs about the game of golf. When frustrated, they'd go back to what they thought were the basics. Several of these beliefs are still thought to be the "right way" to golf. Unfortunately, these techniques and mechanics are not necessarily the best for everyone. Listed below are some examples that may NOT be true in order for you to play your best.

Head down through impact – Keeping your head down through impact restricts motion and makes the body come upward through impact, causing you to top the ball. Take Annika Sorenstam, for example. The LPGA tour player played throughout her career with her head releasing towards the target through impact when hitting the ball. What worked for her may or may not work for others, but it does show that there is more than one way to hit a golf ball.

Left arm straight – For many, this causes tension in the arm. The left arm will straighten at impact when the ball is struck toward your intended target.

I have to have the right club to hit the right shot – You can be creative with your club selection. This means you never have to be between clubs or without the "right" club. The doubt that results from thinking you may not have the right club can interfere with your thought process of hitting the target. Being able to hit with a wide number of clubs will reduce the amount of doubt and time over the ball and build confidence that you will achieve your desired result.

Getting under the ball – By trying to get under the ball, the golfer can actually top the ball during the upswing. We would like to strike down and through the ball, making the divot after impact. The reason why people dig deep into the ground when they hit the ball is because they are stuck there. They are not focused on the target but rather focused on the ball itself.

When people get frustrated on the course, they try to fix it as soon as possible (with techniques like these) rather than seeing the frustration for what it is. It may be better to think about why you are frustrated when it is happening. Did you lose the target, or was it a bad break? What can you do differently the next time?

CREATIVITY

Our ability to play with our creative minds is critical for success. There is an inner knowing that we have this as part of our performance. When I have people play a hole backward, they often play the hole much better that they would the regular way. Why? The perspective changed, and it allowed them to use their creativity. They hit shots they didn't know they had. They also didn't have a good or bad version in their mind of how the situation would turn out. There have been hundreds of four-club tournaments through the years, and many people play the same or better than with their full set.

Our creativity is clearly related to our mental state. When our minds are well-rested, receptive to change, alert, and open to questioning, we are more creative. Pressure and stress can cause a loss of the target and also a lack of creativity. Internal and external stress can also have a huge impact on the outcome of our performance. It is important to deal with physical, mental, emotional, and behavior symptoms of stress in order to achieve top performance.

Take, for example, the feeling of losing someone close to you. The loss can quickly reveal that the expression "a broken heart" can actually become a medical reality with symptoms—changing our eating and sleeping habits as well as our neurological activity, just to name a few. Not to mention, loneliness is a factor that can lead to heart disease. Dealing with stress in positive ways is key to getting your mind back in the game and getting your body healthy to be at your best on the course.

STAY IN THE NOW

Remaining focused on the present moment is critical for top performers in order to play their best under adversity. People can be afraid of telling others what their score is when they are playing well in the round. This is because they are afraid of the distraction of overachieving. If you are already prepared to score low, then this should not matter. We simply get nervous when we are playing our career rounds because we have not rehearsed in our minds how low we can go.

To play "in the now," rather than thinking ahead to the future or back to the past, is important. We use biofeedback to help people understand how to remain in the now. This mindful exercise helps people stay present with clarity and openness to achieve their desired outcomes.

One technique to keep yourself in the moment and not look too far into the future is to announce your target aloud before you hit the ball. (For example: "I am hitting my ball to the base of the tree in the middle of the fairway.") This allows you to stay more focused on one shot at a time, rather than picturing your score at the end of the round. If your voice does not sound committed to the shot, announce your target over again. Analyze the words and determine if they are clear on what you want to achieve and your right to achieve.

Many of us don't notice how little control we have over our mind, whether while playing the game or being off the course. This is because our habits control our mind/energy so well that thoughts seem to follow each other by themselves in an endless flow. For example, when I grew up as a junior golfer, I would find myself playing the same shots on the same course. The basic disorder of my mind would take over, and I would recall the past and repeat it in the present. I needed to change my thoughts by clearly focusing on what I wanted to achieve. I decided I would call the target out loud clearly to regroup and regain a clear intention of my intended target. After doing this, I was amazed at how often my ball would go exactly where I called. It was truly proof how the mind offers as many intense opportunities for creating action as does the body. It was also a great way to learn how mental activity can produce enjoyment. It was clear to me that when the ball floats off line, I have lost the target. The ball goes exactly where we hit it.

Target – What is your target? Defining your target and visualizing a goal.

Focus – The ability to hold the target in your mind throughout the performance, while removing interference.

Relax – relaxing so that you can engage in the moment and detach from the negative emotions

Release – Releasing to achieve your target or goal, with clear intention while unattached to the things you can't control.

Chapter Nine

Reviewing the Outcome with Self-Coaching and Continued Coaching from Others

No matter what the endeavor, reviewing the outcome of any action is a critical component for achieving success. One way to do that is to accept coaching from yourself and others. In business, how do you encourage people to let your organization become flexible to face the issues so you can approach a situation competitively? Golf and business, as well as all things worth doing, involve preparation, action, and review. I have participated in innumerable golf game reviews at the nineteenth hole. Some golfers seem to remember each shot and play them again and again in their minds. Some businesspeople review their performance every day when they get home. How many of us, though, are completely honest about the game we played and the day we had? Are we focusing only on our great shots, or do we only concentrate on where we went wrong? Neither approach will help us look at the reality of how we performed. Instead, we must consider the entire experience to arrive at an accurate conclusion.

Goals are made reality by nonjudgmental feedback. The facilitation of an outside group or individual has been important to my work because it allows people to see and believe in different ways to achieve their peak performance. This also allows participants and spectators to be able to achieve a state of mind that is highly enjoyable. This happens when the goals are challenging in business and sports and we direct our attention to them with proper focus. Creativity and flow result, and they can lead to extraordinary outcomes. This coaching can also provide awareness of how you can be grateful and cherish the things you have and can achieve.

In golf we use the scorecard to help manage our focus. The number of strokes we take is clear and measurable and allows us to let the numbers (instead of personalities, egos, subjective issues, emotions, and other intangibles) rule what is really happening. The scorecard helps everyone remain focused on what matters. Of course, there are many other indicators of success (for example, having fun, getting fit, and enjoying the social side), but those things are difficult to measure and evaluate. Most of us truly have fun when we improve performance of the bottom line, whether it is a lower score in golf or a higher profit in business.

The scorecard allows individuals and businesses to monitor where they are at all times. The numbers help us to remain focused. Learning can only happen when we know how we are doing. It is not a matter of making judgments, such as good or bad or right or wrong, but rather a measuring tool of our progress. With that we can focus on what we can do to make a difference.

In business, people are far less likely to keep score and have much less ability to judge how they have done at the end of a day. How would you rate yourself and your organization on a scale from one to ten on being accountable? Most people rate themselves five or less. In my opinion, this is because most people lose sight of their goals and vision. On the golf course and in business, this so easily happens to us all. Just having a few bad shots in a row or a few mistakes in a day can put us in the mindset of fixing what we did wrong versus shooting with clarity to the target. When we turn our focus away from our target and aim it to what we did wrong, we are shooting in the wrong direction. In either case remaining clear on your goal, or scorecard, will keep you focused on what is most important. Do not take lightly the importance of checking on a regular basis that you are on target. By doing this you can monitor the pulse within yourself and within all levels of an organization, thus keeping everyone in alignment and focused.

Keeping a scorecard will help you to learn how to set goals in your business and in your sport. This will hold you accountable to your results within each ninety-day period. You will learn how to take the pulse of where you and the organization are regarding the goals you are trying to achieve. While most people see meetings as a waste of time, if done correctly, they are a very useful tool. You can learn how to make them productive while creating an enjoyable experience for all.

It is easier to release when you know where it is that you are going. The scorecard you filled out in Chapter 1 is designed to be done on a routine basis every ninety days. It does very little good to only do one and then put it away (like only keeping score on one round of golf and then assuming you know from then on how you are playing). Each time you fill out the scorecard, your overall goals will become clearer. It is unreasonable to think that you can be totally clear within the first ninety-day period.

However, you will begin to see what you are accomplishing and continue to refine your goals and target.

Successful people master playing the game of golf or running a business by operating with a crystal clear vision that is shared by everyone involved. In business they have the right people in the right seats or jobs. On the golf course, they are the ones who know how to play their own game and are clear on how to get the most out of the experience. The release happens when one is clear. These people always know where they are headed and where they stand in relationship to the bottom line. In both golf and business, they choose to play unattached to the outcome. They identify and solve issues promptly in an open and honest environment.

They maintain the goal sheet/scorecard so that everyone can be held accountable. They begin to understand that the mastery is ongoing. These are the people who establish priorities for themselves while coaching others on their team to a high level of trust, communication, and accountability.

THE ROLE OF COACHING

Are you coachable?

A coach is a person who knows what you want and helps you not only believe in the possibilities but also achieve your desired outcomes. The key is for the coach to know what the client wants. In the coaching style that we use at Performance In Motion, we not only need to be good listeners, but we also observe both the client's body and thought process to help him or her become clear. Most people can be trained to take their games to the next level. Even professional athletes and Olympians do not always have the gift of finding enjoyment in pushing themselves beyond the existing boundaries.

If one is not aware, it is hard to make changes. The client needs to assess his or her vision, values, goals, and commitments before any coaching can be applied. In other words, there is no coaching if there is no target. When I was teaching golf full time, I discovered that there were very few people who knew what they really wanted out of the experience of playing golf. Of course, everyone wants to play well, score low, win a match or tournament, or simply look good in front of others. But at the end of the day, most of these people were playing golf as a pattern to interrupt the rest of their lives. A big part of the role of a coach is helping the client to understand what it is that he or she wants from the bigger picture of the whole experience.

To be a coach, one must understand that the genius is in the client, not the coach. Ultimately the coach's job is to help clients become aware of the genius that is inside them so they can focus on the target or goal and let go of any interference or barriers that may be in the way. A coaching session should end with the clients trusting themselves more than the coach. I believe that the ideal role of a coach is to be a mirror for clients and reflect back what is really happening to them. Rather than teaching or telling them how to do something, I like showing them something they didn't know, which strengthens the instinctual knowledge that they already have inside. This nonjudgmental feedback makes their performance improve much faster and last longer.

In Steven Pressfield's entertaining book, *The Legend of Bagger Vance: A Novel of Golf and the Game of Life*, Bagger Vance and Keeler are discussing the natural swing of a player and how it would be impossible for a professional instructor to change a person's swing to fit a preconceived idea of what that swing should look like. "I believe that each of us possesses, inside ourselves," Bagger Vance began, "one true Authentic Swing that is ours alone. It is folly to try to teach us another, or mold us to some ideal version of the perfect swing. Each player possesses only that one swing that he was born with, that swing which existed within him before he ever picked up a club."

Good coaches work with your natural gifts, whether it be your natural swing in golf or your natural strengths in business and life, providing critical guidance only when necessary, rather than forcing you to do something a certain way.

 In the early '90s, I had a client, Jeff, who had a two-and-a-half-year-old son at the time, Kyle, who was learning how to golf. I was teaching golf and just learning how to coach people. Watching this young kid refuse any kind of help and do it on his own was very profound to me. It showed me the value of learning through one's own experience instead of instruction. Good coaches know when to get out of the client's way and let the client learn through his or her own experience. Certainly Jeff had the intention of getting in the way of his son's performance. Kyle was in experimental mode and just wanted to try golf. Below is a series of pictures that show Jeff stepping in to teach Kyle.

Captions: 1) Kyle swings without focus and misses. 2) Dad helps by trying to fix grip, stance, and swing. 3) Kyle becomes mad while being told how to do it, keeping his club away from his dad in preparation for the next shot. 4/5) Swings and misses out of frustration, tossing the club. 6) Lines up, playing his own game with split-hand reverse grip. 7/8) Connects with ball and follows through. Beautiful shot by guided coaching and self discovery.

The first photo shows Kyle lost in focus. He wound up, swung, and missed hitting the ball. In the second photo, his dad saw his frustration and walked over to help. He took hold of Kyle's club so he could show him how to swing, but Kyle pulled away, turned around, and walked over to yet another ball. Being even more frustrated and completely out of it, Kyle swung, missed the ball, and let go of the club. It looked as though he already had that planned in his mind to do that based on the interference that he got from his dad. As he through the club out of his own frustration, Kyle then walked back and tried it again. This time he calmed down, took aim, swung, and made contact with a great shot. Without a single word of instruction or help from his well-intentioned father or me, he hit the next six balls in a row. Even at only two years of age, Kyle learned best from his own experience. Of course there has been some guided instruction along the way but mainly coaching.

It is the experience itself that is the teacher. When I first started teaching golf back in the mid-1980s, I was a golf teacher. I was taught to teach golf, and the expectations of my clients were that they would be told what to do. Along the way, though, I realized just how much of a setup for failure that was. All the education that I had at that time was strictly about grip, stance, and swing. I had never learned about target or mindfulness.

There were many coaches who helped me along this journey, but a combination of Craig Waryan (PGA professional), Jim Early (business coach), Fred Shoemaker (golf coach and author of Extraordinary Golf), and Tim Gallwey (with the inner game methods) shifted my point of view well beyond what I thought was the role of a golf teacher and into the role of a coach. I soon realized how golf, other sports, hobbies, and motion in general can be a very powerful tool for us to make changes in all areas of our lives.

Throughout this book, one of the basic philosophies is to become your own coach as well as accepting coaching from others. These other coaches don't necessarily have to be golf professionals or instructors. There are great coaches all around us. Use your teammates, golf buddies, and work partners to coach you, perhaps asking such simple things as "What is your target?" or "Where is the interference coming from?"

As mentioned, some of my inspiration comes from Timothy Gallwey. Gallwey, author of The Inner Game of Tennis, was working on his new method of coaching using motion techniques in the 1970s. He was challenged by The Reasoner Report to help someone learn how to play tennis while they filmed the first lesson. To make things more interesting, Gallwey was not allowed to pick his student for the live televised event. After dozens of interviews with people who had never played the sport before, the crew of The Reasoner Report chose a woman who was short, overweight, and had no desire to break a sweat to be Gallwey's student. She was very reluctant and even called to cancel, but she eventually showed up at the courts wearing a muumuu (a traditional full-length dress popular in Hawaii).

Gallwey, unfazed by the sight of his new prospect, went right to work, beginning with things the woman already knew how to do from previous experience. As a person hit tennis balls from across the other side of the tennis court to Gallwey, he explained to the woman he simply wanted her to focus on watching the ball bounce. "When the ball bounces," Gallwey said, "I want you to say 'bounce.'" After a few hits, he then added, "When I hit the ball back, I want you to say 'hit.' I'll return a couple of balls, and then you can jump in when you're ready. Again, simply watch the ball and say, 'bounce…hit, bounce…hit, bounce…hit.'"

After three or four swings from Gallwey, the woman jumped in without hesitation, as though she didn't want to miss out on any of the fun. She started hitting the tennis balls back on her own, watching the ball and chanting the mantra "bounce…hit, bounce…hit."

There was no technical jargon, no explanation of how to hold the racquet, no mention of footwork or of stepping forward to return the groundstroke, and no hint of the mechanics taking place. The focus was simply on watching the ball and seeing where she wanted to hit the ball, which the woman knew she could do. After ten or fifteen shots, she was hitting returns consistently back over the net.

Gallwey progressed to the backhand without a single word about how to hold the racquet. He simply said, "Now I want you to keep doing the same thing, but switch to the other side of the racket." Immediately, and quite naturally, she began returning the balls with a backhand stroke. "Bounce...hit," she continued. "Bounce...hit."

For the serve, which is one of the most difficult strokes in tennis for many, Gallwey again focused on the student's past experience to introduce a new skill. He didn't tell her how high to throw the ball, or where she should throw the ball, or how to place her feet. "I want you to think of the serve as a dance that's counted in threes, like a waltz," he said. "One, two, three. One, two, three. Think of a tune you know, and hum it out loud as you count one, two, three. One, two, three. Now throw the ball into the air on count one and hit it on count three." He demonstrated, counting with the woman as he served. "One (toss the ball up), two, three (hit). One, two, three." The woman followed his lead and was serving balls over the net after several attempts. "Keep counting and humming your tune out loud," Gallwey encouraged. "One, two, three. One, two, three."

In twenty short minutes after first walking on the court, this woman who had never played tennis before and had no interest in the sport was excited and energetic, returning shots in her first tennis match. She had none of the tennis lingo or any knowledge of tennis mechanics, but she had enough innate skill in her body to play and enjoy the game because Gallwey began with what she already knew from past experiences. In short, he coached her.

A BALANCE BETWEEN SAFETY AND CHALLENGE

What I've learned from Gallwey and his approach is that good coaches provide just enough safety for their clients to allow them to experiment with new ideas but not so much that they become too comfortable and complacent. If we provide too much challenge and not enough safety, people tend to allow fear to take over and become resistant to exploring new ideas. Instead of becoming comfortable, they become stuck or decide to quit. If we provide too much safety, however, people feel stuck and bored and become unwilling to take risks.

I have observed that this not only occurs in sports but also in business and in life. In the workplace, if one does not have a balance between safety and challenge, it is hard to take on risks that are needed in today's work environment. Too much safety makes for a complacent team. Too much challenge can provide a tremendous amount of stress. It is often the coach's job to provide the safety and challenge when needed so the client focuses or refocuses on the target and conditions.

The role of a great coach is provide safety (target, focus, relax, and release) while still providing challenge.

My role as coach is providing a safe environment, removing any obstacles in the way, and accepting people for who they are. But, at the same time, it is also my role to challenge people and slightly remove the feeling of safety to push them to their potential. A coach encourages and empowers people to excel, believing in them enough to know that they have what it takes to get the job done.

In short, coaching is a balance between safety and challenge. The coach's job is to ask adequate questions so that the client can remain focused on his or her desired outcome. The coach also should provide safety from physical and emotional stresses. For example, Gallwey provided a safe physical environment by having a skilled assistant on the other side of the net hitting balls to the new player rather than having a machine launch balls out at fifty miles per hour. In terms of the emotional environment, Gallwey warmly welcomed his new player rather than belittling her for being out of shape, improperly dressed, or ill-prepared. He embraced her for the unique person she was. As for the challenge, Gallwey never doubted the abilities of his student. He expected her to succeed, and she did. She amazed an entire television audience in just twenty minutes.

It's worth noting that coaching works best when the person wants to be coached and knows what they want to learn before coaching begins. When I work with business owners who wish to take their game to the next level (whether golf or business), they must be ready to do so. Most people are unable to reach the next level because they are simply not ready to let go of the last one. If a person doesn't have the target clearly in mind or if the person doesn't want to hit the target, the person will not succeed.

Perhaps you want to see your business grow or your golf game get better, but at the same time you are frustrated, tired, and unwilling to take on any more risk. The truth is that before you can grow, you need to be clear on what you want to achieve and make a commitment to it. You are abandoning one way of doing things without completely knowing if you are capable of doing things another way. The openness to change should be on your terms, no matter if you are working with a business or team during the process. If one person doesn't buy into what the business or team is doing, it will make it much more difficult for everyone else to succeed. It is the intent of this book to give you tools to reflect and take action upon.

Change may be scary from time to time, but it is also an opportunity to open up to new possibilities. With the right vision, structure, and focus, you can evolve and realize your full potential. To be ready for this change, you need an open mind and a willingness to grow and be vulnerable.

In golf, for example, it's hard to coach someone if they don't know where they want to go. The role of the coach is to help the client fully understand the experience of golf and not just focus on the performance. How are you going to coach yourself, receive coaching, and give coaching?

ASK "WHAT DID I LEARN TODAY?"

As I mentioned in the "Playing the Game" chapter, the coaching I do in my workshops can be as simple as asking the right questions. For example, asking the question "What did you learn today?" rather than "How well did you do?" has prompted a breakthrough for many people. Individuals tend to give up if they perform poorly, thinking they are not good enough to continue in the sport. Asking yourself what you learned is one way to become aware of how to improve in the future.

When you look at your performance objectively by asking what you learned, you will often discover one area that, with a little work, could change your whole game for the better. Like a major league baseball player in a batting slump, it's not an issue of whether you are good enough to continue playing. It may just be an issue of focus or a small adjustment needed to get you back to peak performance. When you look at your performance objectively, being aware of what is actually happening, you can respond appropriately as needed, rather than simply shutting down completely and calling it quits. Remember, if an elite baseball player is batting .300, that means he is failing seven out of ten times at the plate. While failure in business, golf, and other sports certainly isn't fun, it is part of life, and it happens to all great performers. In most PGA golf tournaments, there is only one winner. In the Stanley Cup or the Super Bowl, there is only one team that wins. However, there always seems to be an opportunity to look at a situation and learn from our ups and downs.

Looking at it a little differently, "How well did I do?" immediately goes into good or bad and right or wrong, as though the issue is black and white. It also puts you on the defensive if you didn't do well. It labels your performance rather than allowing you to take an objective look at the big picture. Let's say you just played your best round of golf ever. Asking yourself how well you did has one answer: "Great!" But it ends there. It might also put unrealistic pressure on you the next time you golf, because now you have an even higher goal to achieve than the last time out, which you may think is impossible—in other words, "I played so well I'll never be able to do that again."

Asking "What did I learn?" after the same great score, however, lets you evaluate your golfing performance objectively. For example: "I was able to relax; I was aware of when I was relaxed and what I was thinking during the swing." Being aware of when you were relaxed is something you can repeat, over and over again, which, in turn, will give you confidence that you can play the same or better next time out.

In business, an example could be looking at your actual sales of a particular product for last quarter. Asking how well you did may leave you with one answer: "Poorly." Asking what you learned, however, may help you see that, while sales lagged behind for the product, returns were drastically reduced and customer service was up. Instead of dropping the product, you may discover you simply need a different focus for your marketing campaign to improve sales.

When clients call me before an important meeting or golf match, I remind them to focus on the target and then ask these questions:

What's the best that can happen?
What's the worst that can happen?
What is it you'd like to have happen?

After the meeting or match, I follow up with these questions:

What things happened as you wanted?
What did you become aware of?
What did you learn (rather than how well did you do)?

You can ask yourself the same questions before a presentation, a team meeting, or at the start of a big project. This will help you stay focused during the performance and encourage you to reflect upon and evaluate your experience in a nonjudgmental way. In this way, you are self-coaching at the highest level.

For many of the people coming through my workshops, coaching is part of their job. We all coach in some way. Some of us might be team leaders, some of us parents, some of us have employees, and so forth. My intent is to role model the behavior of a coach, because my experience is that a major interference for decisive managers is the need to demonstrate they are in control, and they do that by directing others instead of helping others to learn.

It is also helpful to recognize that a true leadership team can lead by a number of different approaches. Would you prefer a dictatorship or a vital leadership team? Both methods can work, but most people prefer to be part of healthy teams consisting of people who define their own visions.

DO YOU HAVE STRUCTURE?

Being structured and yet flexible is critical in remaining focused on your goal. Structure helps you to be organized in a way that reduces complexity and creates accountability. I have observed from my work with small companies that the structure of many small businesses is generally loose or nonexistent. Often the company's structure is governed by the owner's personality, fears, or ego.

For golfers, being unstructured means they don't know what they really score, they don't have a goal, and their only plan for improvement is to work harder on grip, stance, and swing. Golfers might work out at the gym but never train their minds along with their bodies.

Being your own self coach (or taking advantage of a good professional coach) and using your scorecard from Chapter 1 on a regular basis will keep you from falling into this trap. For business, golf, sports, or hobbies, this will allow you to implement and imprint a structure that engages and clearly defines the roles and responsibilities.

RECREATE YOUR VISION

Every vision changes with time. I encourage you to redo your vision and your vision board on a regular basis. Take time to ponder each picture and ask yourself if that vision still speaks to you. If it doesn't, there is nothing to stop you from replacing it.

A characteristic of all living things is that we change and grow. Your golf game will not remain static. What you want to shoot at age sixty will likely not be what it was at age thirty. In business, you will find your goals and dreams are quite different when you near retirement than they were when you first started out. Every stage of life is perfect. Enjoy the game!

Conclusion:

Summary of the Discussion

1 – BECOMING AWARE OF THE CURRENT SITUATION

Awareness is the key to making changes and determining what is working and what isn't working to achieve the results that you would like. It is impossible to change when you do not measure where you are and/or where you would like to be. We all have our ups and downs in a given situation, so it is important to be comfortable with vulnerability, both in business and in golf. As weak or soft as this may sound, when you are truly comfortable being exposed to one another, on a team or on the course, you will begin to perform without playing defensively. As a result, you can focus your energy in the moment, with all of your intent on the target.

This can be difficult at times because most top performers have advanced themselves in schooling and sports by being competitive against others and by being protective of their reputations. The biggest challenge for many competitors is how to remain respectful to themselves and others while still remaining clear on who they want to be. By taking a focused approach, you can dramatically accelerate the process in a relatively short order.

Benefits of having awareness of the current situation:

Business:

- Recognizing strengths and weaknesses.
- Recognizing the need for ongoing coaching to prevent dysfunction.
- Improving effectiveness by knowing what needs to be changed.
- Allowing yourself to be vulnerable, while still having self-trust and trust in others.
- Establishing clear goals for what you would really like to achieve.

Personal goals:

- Recognizing strengths and weaknesses.
- Learning about yourself to help you interact with others.
- Evaluating if you are on track to achieving your desired outcomes.
- Knowing what you want to attract toward yourself.
- Health and wellness
- Establishing clear goals for what you would really like to achieve.

Golf:

- Recognizing strengths and weaknesses.
- Recognizing where you are and where you'd like to be with your game.
- Understanding what aspects of your game you want to improve.
- Understanding what has been holding you back from improvement.
- Knowing what you want from the experience.
- Establishing clear goals for what you would really like to achieve.

2 – DISCOVERING THE POSSIBILITIES

Discovering your vision can begin with the power of thought. Many successful people we see in our lives are successful because they have a clear vision. Creating a vision board will give you clarity about what you want to achieve without having to be perfect. The mental images are there to help you accomplish what you desire.

Through the putting exercise, allow yourself to understand what you are thinking and feeling. You will recognize that there are many different ways you can achieve peak performance, both individually and as a member of a team. You can also see how to put new ideas into use. Embrace the learning process and discover what the data and information do for you. Challenge assumptions that are getting in the way.

Benefits of discovering the possibilities:

Business:

- Putting exercise allows you and/or your team to be open to new ideas.
- Learning from others happens through observing their visions.
- Recognizing whether you allow yourself to think creatively.
- Being in the moment—with staff, clients, etc.
- Being in the mindset to live in growth. You're on the planet to grow yourself and others with an open mind, heart, and desire to accomplish the goals set in front of you.

Personal goals:

- Explaining your vision board helps you gain a better understanding of your vision.
- Allowing yourself to achieve what you may not have thought possible.
- Putting exercise helps you recognize if you are stuck in the same habits and what you can change.
- Learning from others happens through observing their visions.
- Recognizing whether you allow yourself to think creatively.
- Being in the moment—with staff, clients, etc.
- Being in the mindset to live in growth. You're on the planet to grow yourself and others with an open mind, heart, and desire to accomplish the goals set in front of you.

Golf:

- Looking differently at the same target can result in higher performance.
- Recognizing your thoughts, feelings, and the object of your focus when you performed at your best will improve your performance in the future.
- Being in the moment—with staff, clients, etc.
- Being in the mindset to live in growth. You're on the planet to grow yourself and others with an open mind, heart, and desire to accomplish the goals set in front of you.

3 – DEVELOPING A FIRM BELIEF IN YOURSELF AND OTHERS

Sometimes interference can be more difficult to see, especially when it comes from the best intentions. However, when the target becomes clear and you develop self-confidence, interference becomes irrelevant, and you can achieve things you never imagined.

Benefits of developing a firm belief in yourself and others:

Business:

- Team develops focus and creates clarity around direction and priorities.
- Entire team is aligned around common objectives.
- Team sees opportunities before competitors do.
- Learn from mistakes.
- Develop clear intention through thought.
- Make changes clearly and directly.
- Understand others on the team.
- Focus on the future while remaining focused on the present.

Personal goals:

- Align self and family with common goals.

- Adapt to change.
- Develop the ability to relate to others' needs.
- Be clear about your intentions.
- Allow for learning.
- Focus on the future while remaining focused on the present.

Golf:

- Have confidence in your personal ability.
- Know the feeling of the natural swing.
- See distractions and interference but don't be affected by them when aiming for the target.
- Let go of the need for perfection.
- Focus on the future while remaining focused on the present.

4 – DEVELOPING FOCUS

Learning through experience can help you direct your focus to the proper areas. For many, the thought is that if you work hard in the office, the bottom line will improve. The same goes for golf—if you work on your golf swing, your scores will get better. As I have said, this is not necessarily true. The club throwing exercise demonstrates that you have a natural swing inside of you that comes out when you are focused on the target. Performance naturally improves when your focus shifts from the process to the target.

Benefits of developing focus:

Business:

- Enjoy success by seeing, feeling, and doing things differently.
- Move beyond individual goals for the good of the team.
- Avoid distractions.

Personal goals:

- Change your focus to the target through your action.
- Focus on the bigger picture.

Golf:

- See the natural swing inside of you through the club throw.
- Focus on target instead of the ball.
- Focus on your swing without the ball so that when the ball is present you can focus on hitting the target.

5 – PARTNERSHIP OF THE MIND AND BODY

All great relationships, whether with the club and the ball, with members of a business or sports team, within a marriage, or within a friendship, require productive conflict in order to grow. Healthy conflict can save time by helping you recognize what is not working and how you can achieve your desired outcome. Defining your vision through mental images can help you see more clearly what is important to you and others.

Benefits of having a partnership between the mind and body:

Business:

- Be open to change.
- Look for connections between thoughts and words.
- Look forward to meetings and group issues.
- Recognize that productive conflict will improve business in the long term.
- Team members work better together when they are aware of each other's visions.
- Extract ideas from all members.
- Get critical topics on the table.

Personal goals:

- Allow productive conflict in order to grow.
- Play your own game; work toward your own vision.
- Believe in your vision while those around you understand your desires.

Golf:

- Become aware between partnership of club and ball.
- Find your authentic swing.
- Mental images provide clarity to performance.
- Become aware of what is real; be consistent in keeping score.

6 – MAPPING YOUR STRATEGY

Defining your role within a company or how you choose to play the hole will save you time and prevent confusion in the future. Having a plan and clear steps to achieve it makes the process much more manageable and the goal more attainable.

Benefits of mapping your strategy:

Business:

- Have a defined strategy with a clear business plan for all team members that carry the plan throughout the business.
- Plan A, Plan B, and Plan C.

Personal goals:

- Mind mapping.
- Clarify possibilities.

Golf:

- Play the hole backward.
- Draw out the hole and connect the dots three different ways to play the hole.

7 – AIMING FOR THE TARGET

The best organizations and players see their paths clearly but still consistently refine them. However, most business owners and golfers do not understand how powerful having and sustaining a clear target can be.

When applied correctly, all members of the organization will be aware of the target and will work together toward it. On the course, the golfer will hold the target through impact with the ball, never losing focus of it throughout the swing.

Benefits of aiming for the target:

Business:

- Change direction without hesitation.
- Align team with common objectives.
- Clarify company direction and priorities.
- Focus time and energy on important issues and let go of "looking good" and politics.
- Retain achievement-oriented employees.
- Minimize individualistic behaviors.

Personal goals:

- Understand health and wellness.
- Establish clear goals with other family members.

Golf:

- Clarify the target (color of flag, flagstick, etc.).
- Understand shape of shot.
- Be aware of interference but focus on target.

8 – PLAYING THE GAME

Commit to make a difference, shifting from self to others or the target. When playing the game, it is most important to first determine what you want from the experience. The game is more enjoyable when your thoughts are focused during your round on what you want to achieve. Strategizing each hole and giving yourself permission to score low are also important steps. Without a plan and self-confidence, you may find yourself lost on the course and struggling in your round. Being aware of your thought process will help you recognize interference and help you shift your thinking to the target. Finally, focus on the present moment when making a shot. Do not think of bad experiences in the past or how you may collapse in the future if you feel you are overachieving. Be sure of yourself when you make each shot.

Lessons learned/ Benefits of playing the game:

Business:
- Give others the benefit before assessing.
- Learn from mistakes.
- Smile and enjoy peaceful places.
- Recognize what happens when you get stuck.
- Take advantage of opportunities.
- Admit weakness.
- Ask for help.
- Accept feedback from others.
- Offer and accept apologies without hesitation.
- Play your own game while working with others.

Personal goals:

- Clarify your direction.
- Move forward without hesitation.
- Deal with letdowns while remaining focused on outcomes.
- Adapt to change when needed.
- Don't constantly compare your performance to the performance of others.
- Play your own game while working with others.

Golf:

- Are you looking in front of or behind the ball?
- Let the past be the past and focus on the target.
- Play your own game while respecting others.

9 – REVIEWING THE OUTCOME WITH SELF-COACHING AND CONTINUED COACHING FROM OTHERS

The experience itself is the teacher. Coaching is a safe environment to explore the changes needed to become a top performer, while dealing with the challenges to make a difference. The safety must come before the challenge. Once the safety is in place, coaches can provide plenty of challenge. The coaching happens through motion. Great coaches work with your natural gifts and help you use them to succeed in several areas of life. They do not force you to do something their way but instead provide critical guidance only when it is necessary to move forward. The coaching will allow for the learning to become real. A dialogue and coaching allows for making a shift and gives you permission to take action.

Benefits of reviewing the outcome and continued coaching:

Business:

- How do you want to be coached?
- Learn from experiences and mistakes.
- Ensure coaching and teaching are balanced between safety and challenge.
- Accept feedback from others.
- Learn from others.

Personal goals:

- How do you want to be coached?
- Learn from experiences and mistakes.
- Ensure coaching and teaching balanced between safety and challenge.
- Accept feedback from others.
- Learn from others.

Golf:

- Let time pass after the experience before evaluating results (don't become too close).

- How would you have coached yourself to achieve better performance next time?
- What tools can you use to overcome future obstacles?
- Breakthrough or breakdown?
- Were you prepared to play?

GET RID OF PERFORMANCE ANXIETY

Do you feel yourself tensing up before an important meeting or presentation? When faced with implementing an important new business initiative, do you find yourself getting nervous about whether or not you can pull it off? When top performance is required, do you relish the challenge or feel like the world is caving in on top of you?

BE AWARE ABOUT ASSUMPTIONS

Sometimes the interference can be more difficult to see, especially when it is accompanied by the best of intentions. One of my clients, for example, volunteered her expertise to help on a strategic planning commission for a religious institution. She was totally committed to helping the organization move in the right direction. As she attended the meetings, however, she realized no one had a vision; there was no clear direction for how the group wanted to proceed. Because of this, the well-meaning ideas contributed by others were nothing more than interference. The target wasn't clear, so it was hard for the group to focus. Looking back, she realized she could have saved a lot of time and frustration before she started by simply asking the group what their vision was.

PRESSURE ON THE FIRST TEE

The same is true in business. You perform better when you're relaxed. As many people discover in my workshops, when they first do an exercise like putting, there is added pressure and tension when trying to put the ball into the hole when other people are watching. It is the fear of performing well or looking good with someone else watching. Ask golfers where they feel the most pressure on the golf course in hitting a good shot, and most will say on the first tee, because that is where other people are waiting and watching. Speaking to groups or giving presentations is one of the greatest fears people have for the same reasons—they are afraid of looking bad or making a mistake in front of others. For these reasons, performing before an audience, whether it's hitting the golf ball or giving a speech to several hundred people, can cause a great deal of anxiety and interference that takes your mind off the target.

WHEN ANXIETY OVERWHELMS

In the early years of my program, I had a few sessions working with an anchorwoman from a Minneapolis news station to help improve her golf game. The real benefit of the program for her, however, was that the motion exercises at my studio, especially the club throw, helped decrease her anxiety while doing the evening news on television.

Instead of focusing on how nervous she was or on how many people were watching her or on trying to duplicate techniques used by her peers, she learned to relax and focus on the target and the things she could control, which was telling the best news story possible. Focusing on the target—in her case, the best news story possible—made her less nervous, more relaxed, and, therefore, more engaged with her audience.

In business, keeping your thoughts on what you want to say—on your message—and listening to the needs of others, rather than on what other people are going to think, will help you relax and remove interference, whether it's in a job interview, asking a question at a team meeting, or giving a keynote presentation.

GETTING STUCK

This brings up several important points. First, when people are under pressure or are performing below their potential because of other reasons, they usually don't realize what's happening. In other words, they know they aren't performing as they should, but they can't explain why. (It's simply that they've lost the target.) The changes are often happening at a subconscious level. When someone is able to identify the changes taking place, however, and can place a finger on the source of interference, as I do by asking questions and coaching, people can then learn to change on their own. When they can begin to pay attention to what's natural and what's unnatural for them in terms of their thoughts and feelings, they can make huge breakthroughs.

One of the challenges of changing how we think about our lives and the challenges we face is that we get caught in the trap of viewing events and experiences in a fixed way. Sometimes negative experiences color our thinking to the extent that it blocks us from doing what we should be doing.

As I continued to see how my approach to coaching in the golf world was helping people to improve in other areas of their lives, I began to work with clients who wanted to focus on professional and business issues, not just their golf game.

Golf is as much a game of the mind as it is a game of skill. That's what people who I coached discovered. The purpose of using the context of golf is that it removes people from the trappings of work. In a completely different setting, it's so much easier to examine how our thinking affects performance. Golf works because you can hit a ball with a club even if you haven't been on a golf course before. And what I focus on is not on the mechanics of how you hit the ball but on where you direct your thinking—from finding your target to focusing and then removing interference that gets in the way of being focused. This experiential learning helps people discover things about themselves and the way they approach situations that is more insightful about their own personal motivation than the common practice of explaining a process and then practicing it.

APPROACHING THE GAME OF GOLF

For the architect of the golf course, the goal is to defend the layout of each hole. Grasses (long and short), plants, trees, forests, sand, and water etc....

A golfer is the attacker. The goal is to find the easiest route to the highly sought after pin that will result in the fewest casualties. The golfer can be aggressive or play it safe, choosing long-ranged or short-ranged weapons, depending on the distance to the green.

The golfer can attack head-on, going through each obstacle, or attack from the air, going over the obstacles. He or she can focus on the distractions and despair at the solid defense or choose to valiantly focus on the target and shot at hand with confidence and determination. Playing your own game is finding the right balance for your shots, deciding whether it is best to be aggressive or to play more defensively, and knowing what you would like to get out of the experience before you choose to play.

The same applies to business challenges you face. When encountering potential hazards or obstacles, you may have to decide "How can we be more aggressive in this situation? How can we best attack?" At other times it could be more prudent to ask, "Is this a time to play it safe and regroup? What strengths can we build on to make it even more difficult for our competition? How can we build on the advantages we already have?"

Why golf? Golf is a sport that has an 85 to 90 percent failure rate, even at a professional level. The thing to ask yourself is, "In the midst of failing can you see the possibilities? Even while dealing with the letdowns?" CEOs learn about team development, coping, and handling failures. Golf is a sport played by more CEOs than any other sport. Imagine if they used golf as the training tool and learning ground rather than golf being a game of good or bad. If you walked off the golf course in the eyes of Performance In Motion, you could ask yourself, "What did I learn today, what new insights did I discover, and how can I apply them to my team?"

"Games are invented to teach about something we consider more important than the game."

"Many things are possible if you believe they are and if you are willing to work daily toward the established goal. Pretty simple, huh? Is it though? There have been many ah-ha moments for me to learn through clients over the past years as a golf professional and business and performance coach. I have had the opportunity to work with many people throughout the years. I have been coaching over the quarter-century mark and have traveled in and out of many corporate offices, small businesses, and top country clubs around the country, as well as my Golden Valley, Minnesota, studio. I have always been amazed by the power of focus. Oftentimes I have heard clients ask if it is still reasonable to achieve their goals. The answer is so shockingly transparent. If you are willing to believe, then we can do the work. It is reasonable to achieve goals if you believe in yourself. There have been so many times that we will see the possibilities at the height of passion. Thus, I believe that finding the activities that challenge you in other areas of life can tie nicely into how you look at another area of life as well." – Dan DeMuth

As a PGA member in 1995, Dan's knowledge about coaching and the game of golf led him to open Dan DeMuth's Better Golf in 1997 where he was recognized for his coaching work with business executives. Dan was named the 2005 Minnesota PGA Teacher of the Year.

Realizing that he was improving much more than just his clients' golf games, Dan changed both the name and nature of his business to Performance In Motion. He has helped scores of individuals and groups discover their unique abilities and strengths both on the course and in the business marketplace.

As the founder of Performance In Motion, Dan DeMuth couples the principles of education and coaching with motion and performance workshops to enable individuals to realize extraordinary results in life and in business.

Dan invites you to please share the opportunities and successes you have endured by applying any of the concepts covered in the book to your life.

You can find me at Dan@performanceinmotion.biz
Facebook: Performance In Motion
Linked In: Dan DeMuth

For future learning and development opportunities please contact us at the above information.

Made in the USA
San Bernardino, CA
18 March 2015